HEGEMONIC INDIVIDUALISM AND SUBVERSIVE STORIES IN CAPITAL MITIGATION

Capital punishment policies in the USA are almost always justified by an individualistic belief in either rational choice or dispositional attribution, which justifies the death penalty either as a deterrent, or for retributive or incapacitative purposes. This book takes an in-depth look at the mitigation process and the use of individualism in the capital sentencing process. The work examines the use of individualistic (hegemonic) and contextualizing (subversive) discourses in the mitigation cases presented by capital defense attorneys and experts from trials in Delaware, and how these discourses were understood, interpreted, and utilized by jurors who served on those trials and by the judges who imposed the final sentences. This in-depth sociological examination of the use of individualizing and contextualizing accounts throughout the entire mitigation process helps to illuminate the challenges involved in structuring a death penalty that is not arbitrary in a culture that is overwhelmed by individualizing discourses, and thus struggles to account for the entrenched racial and economic inequality that is so conducive to lethal violence. In conclusion, it questions the entire premise of the Supreme Court's jurisprudence of death, which rests on a belief that the discretion of decision makers can be "guided" in a way that accounts for contextualizing evidence and will reduce the death penalty's arbitrary and discriminatory application.

Kleinstuber's analysis of the death penalty in Delaware is timely, informative and sobering. Drawing upon the research procedures of the Capital Jury Project, Kleinstuber presents findings from transcript reviews, face-to-face interviews with jurors and, unique to the Delaware component of the Project, judges' sentencing orders. This triangulation of data provides a consistent and ultimately reinforcing picture of how life or death decisions are made. More often than not, the primary consideration is couched in terms of the crime, what the defendant did, with little mention of the lived experiences that brought him to the scene of the crime. This approach calls into question whether these life or death decisions take into account the "frailties of humankind" that, according the US Supreme Court, are to serve as the basis of a "reasoned moral punishment decision." After reading this book, one is left questioning whether decades of tweaking at the margins of the "machinery of death" (Callins v. Collins, 1994, Justice Blackmun dissenting from denial of cert.) have been successful in reducing, let alone eliminating arbitrariness in capital sentencing.

Marla Sandys, Indiana University, USA

To my children, Jaycee and Ethan.
I love you.

Hegemonic Individualism and Subversive Stories in Capital Mitigation

ROSS KLEINSTUBER
University of Pittsburgh at Johnstown, USA

Routledge
Taylor & Francis Group
LONDON AND NEW YORK

First published 2014 by Ashgate Publishing

Published 2016 by Routledge
2 Park Square, Milton Park, Abingdon, Oxon OX14 4RN
711 Third Avenue, New York, NY 10017, USA

Routledge is an imprint of the Taylor & Francis Group, an informa business

British Library Cataloguing in Publication Data
A catalogue record for this book is available from the British Library.

The Library of Congress has cataloged the printed edition as follows:
Kleinstuber, Ross, author.
Hegemonic individualism and subversive stories in capital mitigation / by Ross Kleinstuber.
pages cm.—(Law, justice and power)
Based on author's dissertation (doctoral)—University of Delaware, 2011, issued under title: "Everyone has choices": constructing individualism in the cultural and institutional life of capital mitigation
Includes bibliographical references.
ISBN 978-1-4724-2559-1 (hardback) 1. Capital punishment—Social aspects—United States. 2. Extenuating circumstances—United States. 3. Sentences (Criminal procedure)—United States—Decision making. I. Title.
KF9227.C2K58 2014
345.73'0773—dc23

2013043675

ISBN 9781472425591 (hbk)

Contents

Acknowledgments

There are numerous people and organizations that have assisted me in completing this book and deserve my gratitude. Most importantly, I would like to thank my beautiful and intelligent wife, Elizabeth Mansley. Without her love, support, and commitment to parenting our children while I completed this book, I never could have written it. She has sacrificed more than I can imagine, and for that I am truly grateful. I also would like to thank Professors Benjamin Fleury-Steiner, Aaron Fichtelberg, and Eric Rise of the University of Delaware and Professor Sandra Jones of Rowan University. Your comments, feedback, and critiques during the data collection process and while working on earlier versions of this project proved invaluable. The work of Professor Judith Ritter of Widener Law School, her secretary Vanessa Gosa, and her law student Ross Flockerzie were also indispensable for sampling, contacting jurors, completing interviews, and acquiring trial transcripts.

I am also indebted to several members of the Delaware court system, who proved quite helpful. Chief Justice Myron T. Steele of the Delaware Supreme Court gave permission to contact and interview jurors. I am grateful to the attorneys who made sentencing hearing transcripts available to me: Keisha Hudson of the Philadelphia Federal Defender's Office, Michael Modica, and Jennifer Kate Aaronson. The staffs of the Kent and New Castle County Prothonotary's Offices were exceptionally accommodating and incredibly helpful. Lisa Robinson, who was then the prothonotary of Kent County directed to the availability of capital sentencing opinions on the state judiciary's website, and Sharon Agnew, New Castle County prothonotary, and her staff—particularly Shawn Lavalee and Mike Monti—took the time to locate and photocopy sentencing opinions that had not been placed on the Internet and allowed me to take up space in their office to read through and take notes on trial transcripts that were not available through other means.

The assistance of the staff members of the Capital Jury Project (CJP) cannot be overstated. Professor William Bowers welcomed me as a member of the project, offered wonderful advice for helping me to get started, assisted me in applying for the Proteus Action League grant that assisted with this research, and read countless drafts of different sections of this book. Professor Thomas Brewer of Kent State University was responsible for acquiring and providing transcriptions of all the interviews conducted, and Christopher Kelly was integral as liaison between myself and the Hindelang Research Center, where the CJP is currently housed. Of course, this project never would have been possible without the 35 jurors who graciously agreed to take time out of their busy lives to share their stories with me (or with Mr. Flockerzie). Therefore, I would like to extend a special thank you to those 35 gracious men and women. Due to confidentiality agreements, they cannot be identified by name, but their contributions were invaluable to this project.

Lastly, I must thank all of those who provided funding for this project: the Department of Sociology and Criminal Justice at the University of Delaware, the Proteus Action League, and the National Science Foundation, through NSF Grant #SES-0520487.

List of Abbreviations

ABA	American Bar Association
ADHD	Attention Deficit Hyperactivity Disorder
CJP	Capital Jury Project
CJP3	Capital Jury Project, Phase III
DOJ	Department of Justice
LWOP	Life Without Parole

Introduction
American Individualism and Capital Punishment

"The only way to stop a bad guy with a gun is a good guy with a gun."
—Wayne LaPierre, NRA Executive Vice President (CBS DC, 2012)

"Acts of monstrous criminality stand on their own. They begin and end with the criminals who commit them ..."
—Former Republican Vice Presidential Candidate Sarah Palin (2011)

"If you don't have a job and you're not rich, blame yourself!"
—Former Republican Presidential Contender Herman Cain (Shahid, 2011)

There is a longstanding belief in the United States that criminals are fundamentally different from law abiding citizens and that the blame for their behaviors can be found solely in their individual choices. Scheingold (1984) refers to this notion as the "myth of crime and punishment," and it has achieved widespread acceptance in American culture. According to this myth, "[C]rime is a rather straightforward problem whose diagnosis and treatment are embodied in widely accepted and universally understood moral truths" (Scheingold, 1984, p. 59). Crime is a result of bad people who are fundamentally different from everyone else (as opposed to say, the result of normal people acting within a given set of social circumstances), and punishment is the appropriate response to criminal behavior because it "is both morally justified and practically effective" (Scheingold, 1984, p. 60). The cultural roots on which this myth rests stretch deep into the American psyche: vigilantism and individual responsibility (Scheingold, 1984, p. 61). Individualistic outlooks on crime and criminals lead to what Haney (1995) calls the "myth of demonic agency"—a view of crime and criminals that de-contextualizes criminal behavior, trivializes the vital role of criminogenic social forces, and assumes that offenders coldly calculate their crimes. In this worldview, there is no reference to the social, economic, and political conditions in which criminal (and non-criminal) choices are embedded, enabled, or constrained. Therefore, those who choose to commit crimes, especially violent felonies such as murder, are simply "bad people" who cannot be rehabilitated. In other words, in commonsense understandings of crime, there is no reference to mitigating circumstances, which are indispensable to the fair, rational, and non-arbitrary operation of capital punishment (*Eddings v. Oklahoma*, 1982; *Gregg v. Georgia*, 1976; *Penry v. Lynaugh*, 1989; *Woodson v. North Carolina*, 1976).

Although cultural depictions of crime serve to reinforce individualistic causal explanations, individualism stretches beyond understandings of criminal behavior and pervades all aspects of American life. The central thesis of American individualism is that everyone is responsible for his or her own fate. One's actions and outcomes are solely the result of the choices one has made; the broader societal context in which those choices are made is trumped or made altogether irrelevant. The fact that everyone has different opportunities, formative experiences, and life histories is rendered insignificant in this account. Rather, actions represent one's character. Individualism often becomes the default causal explanation for everything, including one's socio-economic status, and impacts the ways in which Americans understand and attempt to deal with social problems. In fact, the idea of individual responsibility is so widely and uncritically accepted that it is rarely questioned, leading some to argue that individualism has become hegemonic (Dunn and Kaplan, 2009). Yet, there is another story to be told here—a subversive one that challenges the accuracy of the hegemonic narrative. This subversive tale is illustrated well by the rock band Rise Against (2011), whose song "Disparity by Design" points out the fallacy of individualism's basic tenets while simultaneously acknowledging the power of hegemonic individualism to perpetuate inequality by fooling the poor into blaming themselves for their own predicaments rather than challenging the power of the dominant classes. Both the hegemonic story of individual responsibility and the subversive tale of social causation are important for understanding the workings of capital punishment in America—an institution that is both supported by individualism and serves to symbolically reinforce individualistic causal explanations in American culture (Dunn and Kaplan, 2009; Sarat, 2001; Sarat, 2005); this is especially true in the realm of capital mitigation, which is specifically designed to offer a worldview that competes with the traditional individualistic focus of criminal processing (*California v. Brown*, 1987; Cheng, 2010; *Rompilla v. Beard,* 2005; *Wiggins v. Smith*, 2003; *Williams v. Taylor*, 2000). Yet, there has been no extensive, in-depth analysis of the mitigation process, of the ways in which cultural themes like individualism infect the mitigation process, or the ways mitigation can serve as a site for challenging hegemonic discourses. This book takes advantage of a unique capital sentencing law in Delaware that relegates jurors to an advisory role to examine the ways in which mitigation is presented by defense attorneys and mitigation experts and the ways in which this evidence is utilized in the decision-making process of both lay-jurors and judicial elites.

Dunn and Kaplan's Theory of Hegemonic Individualism

Antonio Gramsci's (1971) conception of hegemony represents a break from traditional conflict perspectives that viewed the powerful as maintaining control through coercion or the threat of starvation. Instead, Gramsci (1971) believed that control was maintained through consent, which elites are able to derive by controlling a culture's messages and images and promoting messages that get the subordinate classes to believe in or support ideologies that actually benefit the wealthy and powerful. The control of a culture's messages is accomplished by educating the masses—either through the formal educational system, through the court system, or through "a multitude of other so-called private initiatives" such as the media (Gramsci, 1971, p. 258). Once the ruling class has gotten certain cultural forms to predominate over others, they have accomplished hegemony (Said, 1978), and through these cultural messages, elites are able to get subordinate classes to internalize certain ideas, thereby causing those groups to accept those ideas without questioning them, even if they are negatively impacted by the resulting policies and beliefs. Questioning them would be like questioning that the sun rises in the east or that water flows downhill—the ideas seem normal or natural and therefore beyond debate. In this way, hegemonic narratives ensure that "those who are supposed to be coerced or oppressed by a system of laws imposed upon them by a ruling minority often seem unaware of their coercion or oppression. Indeed, they are frequently among the strongest partisans of the existing legal system" (Vago, 2012, p. 326).

Dunn and Kaplan (2009) have argued that the idea of individual responsibility is one of these themes that has become so engrained in American culture and institutions that it is rarely questioned and thus forms a commonsense understanding of the world that has achieved hegemonic status. The Founding Fathers were strongly influenced by Enlightenment principles that idealized rationality and the idea of individual free will but overlooked the influence of social forces. The entire American political experiment is therefore based upon the idea that only individuals matter; since only individuals can suffer and only individuals have rights, Americans learn from an early age that the individual is "the ultimate unit of analysis" (Dunn and Kaplan, 2009, p. 342). The concept of individual liberties that most Americans hold dear is based on this conception of individualism, and individualism is the philosophical justification behind *laissez-faire* capitalism. The flip side of individual rights and individual freedom is individual responsibility, in which one's behavior and life outcomes are solely the result of one's own agency. In a capitalist society, the construction of an individualist ethic in which everyone is solely responsible for their life outcomes clearly benefits the dominant classes, who have a greater ability to achieve economic success and exercise power over others. This ethic does not benefit the great majority of people who are not abundantly wealthy and spend their days working for someone else's profit. Nevertheless, since individualism became enshrined in the nation's founding document and gets venerated by most social institutions, Americans tend to internalize this message, which causes individualistic explanations to become the default response for most people and causes the existing social order to appear just—even to the masses who do not benefit.

This message also receives constant reaffirmation in modern society, particularly through the media (Beckett and Sasson, 2004; Haney, 1997; Haney, 2003), who have "become the primary socialization agent by which views about crime and punishment are imbued" (Haney, 1997, p. 317). The extant literature suggests that the media over-rely upon the state's version of events when reporting crime, that they quote the police and the prosecutors more often than defense attorneys, and that the resulting image they construct is one of individual defendants who do not have social histories (Barlow et al., 1995; Chermak, 1994; Condit and Selzer, 1985; Ericson et al., 1991; Gorelick, 1989; Haney, 1995; Haney, 2005; Haney and Greene, 2004; Surette, 1998; Surette and Richard, 1995). The news media typically ignore social and economic context when reporting crime stories (Barlow et al., 1995; Haney, 2003; Humphries, 1981), and in crime dramas, the focus is almost always on the lawbreaker's personal traits with little, if any, attention given to the social circumstances that may have produced his or her criminal behavior (Beckett and Sasson, 2004; Haney, 1995; Haney, 2005). This media portrayal of crime distorts reality in a manner that ignores social context, amplifies myths about crime and criminals, and impedes lucid thinking about capital punishment (Haney, 1997; Haney, 2005). As Haney explains, "Television criminals are depicted uniformly without context, life connections, social relationships, basic human needs, wants, or hardships" (1995, p. 550).

Because of the constant support that individualism receives in American society and its long-standing and deep-rooted nature, it is not surprising that studies show that Americans are more accepting of dispositional causal explanations than environmental ones, especially when it comes to crime. For example, focus group research by Sasson (1995) found that criminal justice leniency was cited as the cause of crime more often than social factors. Although some surveys suggest that Americans often do identify environmental factors as the cause of crime (Beckett and Sasson, 2000, p. 137), individual disposition is more recognized as a causal factor (Flanagan, 1987), and there has been a marked return to individualistic explanations of crime since the challenges offered to this perspective by the leftist movements of the 1960s. By the 1980s, there was "an increased tendency to locate the origin of crime in a person's will rather than in his or her social surroundings" (Cullen et al., 1985, p. 324). Throughout the 1990s, surveys found that despite declining crime rates support for harsher punishments was increasing (Beckett and Sasson, 2000), which suggests that Americans view crime as a rational process that can be deterred or as the result of evil-doers who deserve harsher punishments.

These realities impact the American legal system as well. As Gramsci explained, courts play an important "negative educative function" in constructing hegemonic tales (1971, p. 258). Because the American justice system was formed in the nineteenth century, when Enlightenment ideals and "psychological individualism" were the dominant intellectual frameworks, American legal culture was greatly influenced by the same basic assumptions that fueled the growth of capitalism and liberal political theory; therefore, it was designed to handle questions of individual rather than social responsibility (Haney, 1982; Hurst, 1956). "The theory of behavior embodied in the law," therefore, became "that a crime is the act of a voluntary and responsible agent who chooses between the lawful and the unlawful" (Haney, 1982, pp. 207, 209). Consequently, court procedures are aimed at assigning blame to individuals for harms caused; they are not equipped to grapple with issues related to social causation, which suggests that courts will indeed reinforce individualistic understandings of human behavior. "The essential question posed for professionals is how to deal with an endless stream of individual defendants. Moreover, the legal values that are supposed to guide criminal-process professionals lead in equally individualistic directions" (Scheingold, 1991, p. 25). Since only individuals are subject to crime control agencies, professionals, including judges, attorneys, and mitigation experts, are directed toward considering the fate of individuals divorced from their social circumstances and life histories (Scheingold, 1991, p. 26). This leads "legal decision-makers to ignore most of the racial, socioeconomic, and social psychological differentials that play such a crucial role in the etiology of crime ..." (Haney, 2003, p. 469). Sentencing judges are not in a position to respond to or deal with existing social realities; they are there to dispose of individuals; the same is true of other criminal justice experts. Even if they wanted to deal with structural issues, they would be unable to do so (Scheingold, 1991, pp. 26-7).

These realities exist in both the civil and criminal justice systems, but its influence is perhaps most poignant in death penalty trials. As Dunn and Kaplan put it, "[I]ndividualism is so embedded in our social interventions and the law that it is impossible to talk about particular subjects in capital cases without reinforcing and valorizing it ..." (2009, p. 339). No case illustrates this more starkly than *McCleskey v. Kemp* (1987), where the Supreme Court denied the relevance of compelling evidence of state-wide racial discrimination in the application of Georgia's death penalty because McCleskey could not prove that he personally suffered discrimination in his specific case. Although the creation of a bifurcated capital trial process in *Gregg v. Georgia* (1976) was supposed to create a more contextualized approach to capital sentencing, Dunn and Kaplan (2009) suggest that the hegemonic influence of individualism makes that hope an impossibility. Because of cultural priming, capital jurors enter the courtroom "predisposed to posit violent acts as the product of an odd combination of equally free and unencumbered evil choices, on the one hand, and monstrously deranged, defective traits, on the other" (Haney, 2003, p. 470). From this perspective, it should come as no surprise that capital jurors have difficulty even comprehending the concept of mitigation (Haney and Lynch, 1994; Haney and Lynch, 1997; Lynch and Haney, 2000), let alone applying it in their cases (Brewer, 2004; Haney et al., 1994; Sandys and McClelland, 2003). If one is individually responsible for his or her acts regardless of the environment that may have had radical consequences for early childhood development and moral growth, thus constraining the available options, the presentation of evidence designed to shift responsibility away from the convicted defendant makes no sense. This constraint compels defense attorneys, who are supposed to be contextualizing their clients' behaviors, to rely upon (and therefore reinforce) individualistic themes (Dunn and Kaplan, 2009). After all, if popular discourse and understandings of crime do not acknowledge mitigating structural forces, with what are defense attorneys left to work when constructing their mitigation cases?

It is important to note that conceptions of individualism can take many forms; in fact, respect for the individual's rights is a key reason that Beccaria (1777)—the intellectual father of modern deterrence theory—opposed the use of capital punishment. However, the hegemonic individualism that pervades American culture is one that "relies on microlevel theories of human behavior—people commit crime because they choose to do so or because they lack the necessary moral training, intellectual ability, neurological wiring, or emotional control not to" (Dunn and Kaplan, 2009, pp. 363-4). In other words, the type of individualism that Dunn and Kaplan (2009) see as exerting a hegemonic force on American culture is one that focuses on individualistic explanations for behavior. This vision of individualism depicts humans as the sole causal agents and understands their behaviors and motivations solely through the micro-level of analysis. The problem with this conception is not that it is wrong, *per se*. Human beings do possess the ability to choose their own behaviors and therefore can be held accountable for their behavior. The problem with this version of individualism is that it is incomplete because it ignores the macro-level, contextual, environmental influences on human behavior. Although human beings may possess free will, the decisions they make are made in a social environment that constrains their available options and affects their perceptions of potential courses of action. Therefore, the hegemonic form of individualism that pervades American culture "is problematic because it ignores the sociocultural aspects of being human" (Dunn and Kaplan, 2009, p. 364) and therefore fails to provide a comprehensive understanding of human behavior or life outcomes.

Ewick and Silbey's Sociology of Narrative

Tales, however, are not universally hegemonic. The stories people tell sometimes contain subversive themes that challenge the taken-for-granted assumptions of the cultural master narrative. According to Ewick and Silbey, "narratives can function to sustain hegemony or, alternatively, subvert power" (1995, p. 200). In other words, it cannot be assumed that the stories told by mitigation experts, defense attorneys, jurors, and judges will necessarily reflect and reiterate the theme of individual responsibility. This is one possibility, but it is also possible that mitigation serves as a site for challenging the hegemonic force of individualism.

As Ewick and Silbey (1995) explain, the meaning and telling of stories are affected by the social and historical contexts in which they are told. They are "socially organized phenomena," but stories are told at different times in different ways with different goals and content. Thus, stories can produce different outcomes. Therefore, on the one hand, narratives are "likely to bear the imprint of dominant cultural meanings and relations of power," and "the stories and accounts that are told to and by litigants, clients, lawyers, jurors, and other legal actors are not simply reflective of or determined by those dominant meanings and power relations. They are implicated in the very *production* of those meanings and power relations" (Ewick and Silbey, 1995, p. 211). By being repeated by countless individuals, master narratives become immune to critique and part of the cultural commonsense (Ewick and Silbey, 1995). They simply come to be taken-for-granted as natural and normal (Comaroff and Comaroff, 1991). This is particularly true in the legal world, which is focused on "individualized justice and case-by-case processing" that ends up achieving "a kind of radical individuation" (Ewick and Silbey, 1995, p. 217). On the other hand, however, subversive stories that challenge the dominant ideology and existing power structures can also be told. These subversive stories illustrate the way experiences are part of the larger social world beyond the individual and may give voice to marginalized populations who are unable to find expression in the cultural master narrative. They may clarify the interconnections between the individual and social structure and therefore liberate the teller or the listener (Ewick and Silbey, 1995).

In fact, Ellis (1993) argues that it is too simplistic to describe American culture as purely individualistic because there are numerous examples throughout American history of groups that challenged individualism and focused on group well-being. Rather than a purely individualistic and capitalist worldview usually attributed to the Founders, Ellis (1993) argues that American history has exhibited a balance between community and the individual and that there have actually been five competing political cultures: competitive individualism, egalitarian community, hierarchical collectivism, atomized fatalism, and autonomous hermitude. He suggests that individualistic and communitarian ideas actually co-exist in American culture and that neither is dominant. After all, there are some empirical studies that seem to contradict the hegemonic story. Although it has been found that Americans' views on crime seem to be shifting in more individualistic directions, unemployment and poverty have still been identified as important causes of crime (Flanagan, 1987), and most Americans support alternatives to incarceration, such as spending money to solve social problems (Beckett and Sasson, 2000). Some surveys even find that environmental factors are more likely to be identified as the cause of crime by respondents (Beckett and Sasson, 2000; Sasson, 1995).

The Current Study

Because capital mitigation presents attorneys and witnesses "with a rare legal opportunity to test the law's commitment to individualism" by providing "an opportunity to subvert individualism's dominance by telling *truly* contextualizing tales" (Dunn and Kaplan, 2009, p. 363), Ewick and Silbey's (1995) theory suggests that capital mitigation could help to substantiate individualism or may serve to challenge its accuracy and cultural dominance. Yet, the role of individualism in capital sentencing outcomes and mitigation in particular has never been examined. Dunn and Kaplan argue "that the role of individualism in the life of capital punishment is essential for understanding it as a social fact" (2009, p. 339). Therefore, this study offers a detailed, in-depth analysis of mitigation from its initial presentation at trial to the decision-making processes of capital jurors and judges in order to determine "what is happening on the ground in capital mitigation" (Dunn and Kaplan, 2009, p. 365) and to evaluate whether the capital sentencing trial serves as a site that challenges commonsense understandings of crime and criminality or simply reinforces them. This project is guided by several research questions that have never been answered: Do the taken-for-granted popular explanations of criminality hamper defense attorneys and experts in a way that forces them to downplay the significance of environment and perpetuate individualistic explanations? "What kinds of arguments are practitioners using and why? … Are practitioners attempting what we believe might be *truly* contextualizing stories? If so, how are these stories understood by courts and juries?" (Dunn and Kaplan, 2009, p. 365). That is, how do fact-finders (jurors and judges) respond to the arguments made by capital defense teams during a sentencing trial? As Dunn and Kaplan put it, "Are there tools outside of the psy-complex that could be used to avoid death sentences while simultaneously combating destructive individualism? Or is our legal system so fundamentally individualizing that it is incapable of hearing other accounts of the human experience?" (2009, p. 363).

In order to get a complete picture of the mitigation process and a more complete understanding of how this process relates to individualism in American culture, these questions must be explored. To try to offer a preliminary answer to these questions, this study will take an in-depth look at the mitigation process in Delaware, a state that vests final capital sentencing authority in trial judges. To begin this exploration (and this study is just a beginning), this research relies on three data sources: transcripts of capital penalty trials, interviews with former capital jurors, and the written sentencing opinions of trial judges. This approach advances the knowledge of capital mitigation in at least three ways. First, it seeks a comprehensive understanding of the way in which mitigating evidence is actually presented in specific trials and how its presentation relates to broader cultural messages. Second, and relatedly, it incorporates trial transcripts, which permits a comparison of what fact-finders described as important to the evidence actually presented at trial. Lastly, this study brings trial judges' decisions to the forefront. The sentencing decisions of judges in capital trials have yet to be examined, but as judicial elites, they have tremendous power both to construct and to challenge hegemonic discourses.

This book begins with a review of existing knowledge on mitigation and capital sentencing decision making and then describes how this study will expand on this literature, what it investigates, and the methods used for collecting and analyzing the data. In Chapter 2, I explore the ways in which mitigation is trapped by hegemonic individualism and thus reinforces individual responsibility as a cultural norm. Specifically, in every case in this sample, defense attorneys and experts argued that the defendant lacked the culpability requisite for a death sentence and that life without parole would both protect the community and be sufficient punishment for the defendant's crime. In Chapter 3, mitigation's subversive potential is explored. In six of the eight cases in this sample, defense attorneys used the defendant's life and social history in an attempt to mitigate the offense and contextualize his behavior. They offered a competing theory of human behavior that stressed the causal importance of external environmental forces, and five of these cases used expert witnesses to make the connection between prior experiences and subsequent behavior explicit. Furthermore, attorneys in all eight cases used the testimony of friends or family members of the defendant to show that the defendant is embedded in a web of social relationships, that he is capable of good deeds, and that his family would be adversely affected by his execution. In Chapter 4, the sentencing decision-making processes of the jurors on these cases and their receptivity to mitigating evidence are examined via in-depth interviews. Overall, the jurors based their sentencing decisions almost entirely on culpability and rejected the relevance of contextualizing mitigation that did not have some direct nexus to the crime. In some cases, the jurors were even overtly hostile to the defense's use of contextual mitigation. In Chapter 5, the judges' sentencing opinions are analyzed. Again, the sentencing rationale of judges rested almost entirely on culpability and either ignored or downplayed the relevance of environmental forces. Although the judges would occasionally mention the structural mitigation presented by the defense, rarely did they consider such evidence in their sentencing decisions. In fact, in only one case did the judge appear to seriously consider factors unrelated to the crime. Finally, in the concluding chapter, the findings of this study and their implications for both theory and public policy are examined. After describing some of the limitations of this study, I also explain how the findings of this study, combined with knowledge from prior research, suggest the death penalty needs to be abolished. Cultural forces are likely to influence the death sentencing process in a way that impedes full understanding of the social forces that affect human behavior and prevents full consideration of mitigation. Without proper consideration of mitigation, the death penalty cannot be implemented in a fair and even-handed manner and will therefore remain arbitrary and capricious.

Chapter 1
Individualism and Capital Sentencing: What We Know and What We Hope to Learn

As Dunn and Kaplan put it, "Law and society scholars have theorized about the link between capital punishment and the hegemony of individualism, but few offer empirical investigations to illustrate how individualism makes capital punishment possible (and *vice versa*) in the contemporary United States" (2009, p. 337). They attempt to demonstrate the link between individualism and capital sentencing through an in-depth investigation of a single mitigation case in a southern state that looks at the social interventions one capital defendant received as a child and the framing of his problems by his defense team. Yet, a single case study, while critically important for constructing theoretical claims and illuminating the ways culture and the law affect each other, still leaves many unanswered questions. Is this case representative or anomalous? Furthermore, Dunn and Kaplan (2009) do not attempt to decipher how mitigating stories are understood by fact-finders. Although the Capital Jury Project and other studies provide insight for how jurors come to their sentencing decisions, there has been little attempt in the literature to compare the decision-making process of jurors to actual court transcripts, and there have been no modern efforts to analyze the way *judges* make decisions in capital sentencing cases when they are given final sentencing authority. It is for these reasons that this study is necessary. This study follows eight mitigation cases throughout their life in court: what types of arguments do defense attorneys and experts present to judges and juries, and how do those same fact-finders respond to those arguments? Although eight trials from a single state are incapable of being generalized, the use of multiple cases helps to illuminate some patterns that may exist, and this study is more in-depth than Dunn and Kaplan's (2009) because it also attempts to determine how fact-finders interpret mitigating evidence. At the same time, it expands the literature on juror behavior by incorporating trial transcripts that allow the responses of jurors to be compared to the evidence actually presented at trial, and it expands the literature on death sentencing to include the sentencing decisions of *judges*.

Mitigation and the Supreme Court

"Capital mitigation presents a unique site for studying the law's relationship to individualism" (Dunn and Kaplan, 2009, p. 363) because defense attorneys are granted wide latitude to present any type of mitigating evidence they want and the Supreme Court actually *expects* this presentation to include contextualizing environmental evidence. The Supreme Court made this clear when it ruled that mandatory death penalty statutes are unconstitutional in *Woodson v. North Carolina* because sentencers are required to consider the "diverse frailties of humankind" (1976, p. 304). Combined with the Court's decision in *Gregg v. Georgia* (1976), this ruling helped create the guided discretion statutes that are supposed to give sentencers a clear set of rules for choosing between a life and a death sentence and thus are supposed to eliminate arbitrariness in the death sentencing process. Since the re-authorization of the death penalty in 1976, the Supreme Court has stressed that a key part of the constitutionality of these guided discretion statutes is a full consideration of *mitigating* circumstances that could be used to support a sentence less than death, and it has recognized the integral role that environmental influences from the defendant's life and social history play in considerations of mitigation.

In capital penalty trials, the defendant must be treated as a "uniquely individual human being" (*Woodson v. North Carolina*, 1976, p. 305) and limitations may not be placed on the types of mitigating evidence defendants may present or sentencers may consider (*Lockett v. Ohio*, 1978). Not only is what qualifies as relevant mitigation nearly limitless but sentencers in capital cases may not "refuse to consider, *as a matter of law*, any relevant mitigating evidence" (*Eddings v. Oklahoma*, 1982, p. 114). This relevant mitigating evidence includes environmental influences that bear no direct nexus to the crime: "the background and mental and emotional development of a youthful defendant [must] be duly considered in sentencing" (*Eddings v. Oklahoma*, 1982, p. 116). At the heart of guided discretion is "a reasoned moral response to the defendant's background, character, and crime" (*California v. Brown*, 1987, concurring opinion, p. 545; adopted by the Court's majority in *Penry v, Lynaugh*, 1989), and *full* consideration of mitigating evidence is "essential" to this reasoned moral response (*Penry v. Lynaugh*, 1989), which means that sentencers must actually take *all* mitigating evidence into consideration when deciding on a sentence—including those related to the defendant's past. "The sentencing process is fatally flawed," according to the Court, when sentencers are "not permitted to give meaningful effect or a 'reasoned moral response' to a defendant's mitigating evidence" (*Abdul-Kabir v. Quarterman*, 2007, p. 264). In other words, the Supreme Court has ruled that the constitutionality of the death penalty rests on an assumption that sentencers will consider not just the facts of the crime but the environmental influences beyond the control of the convicted killer as well.

In an attempt to ensure that such considerations take place, the Supreme Court has ruled that defendants have a right to challenge for cause any automatic death juror because such jurors would fail to give proper consideration to aggravating and mitigating evidence (*Morgan v. Illinois*, 1992). The Supreme Court has even concurred with the position espoused by the American Bar Association (ABA) (2003; 2008) that the effective presentation of capital mitigation requires an extensive background investigation that explores the defendant's life and family history. According to the ABA capital defenders need "to illustrate and illuminate the factors that shaped and influenced the client's behavior and functioning" including the "long-term consequences of deprivation, neglect and maltreatment during developmental years; social, cultural, historical, political, religious, racial, environmental and ethnic influences on behavior…" (2008, pp. 682-683). It is the function of a capital defense to team "to explain a client's life through the comprehensive process of compiling a social history, thereby revealing the client's humanity and providing important context for the client's conduct at the time of the crime" (Holdman & Seeds, 2008, pp. 883-884). In 2000, the Supreme Court ruled that the failure of trial counsel to investigate evidence of extreme family dysfunction fell below an objective standard of reasonableness (*Williams v. Taylor*, 2000), and it has since instructed capital defense attorneys that competent and effective assistance of counsel in death penalty cases *requires* them to conduct a thorough investigation of the defendant's past (*Rompilla v. Beard*, 2005; *Wiggins v. Smith*, 2003). Yet, some states still required mitigating circumstances to have some nexus to the crime, so in *Tennard v. Dretke* (2004), the Court rejected the nexus test, reiterated its holding in *Eddings* that "virtually no limits are placed on the relevant mitigating evidence" (1982, p. 114), and insisted that defendants do not need to establish a nexus between their crimes and the mitigating circumstances presented.

These rulings indicate that the Supreme Court considers mitigating evidence to be highly contextual and multifaceted because contextual evidence of the defendant's prior experiences can help sentencers to understand how or why a convicted murderer came to his murderous actions, which is relevant and important for determining sentence in capital cases. As stated in the concurring opinion in *California v. Brown*, defendants whose criminal actions "are attributable to a disadvantaged background, or to emotional and mental problems, may be less culpable than defendants who have no such excuse" (1987, p. 545). All of this suggests that from a legal standpoint, capital mitigation is supposed to stand in contrast to the highly individualized nature of American legal culture and recognize that just because humans have the ability to exercise free will does not mean that their choices are completely autonomous. Humans may be rational creatures, but our decisions and actions are also greatly impacted by the social structures and cultural realities surrounding us. The Supreme Court's rulings indicate that these influences should be considered when capital defendants are sentenced.

The Presentation of Mitigating Evidence

Despite the constitutional dictates of the Supreme Court, Dunn and Kaplan believe that because of the power of hegemonic tales, "it is practically impossible to talk about particular subjects in capital cases without reinforcing and valorizing" individualism. This includes capital defense attorneys who will "inadvertently reinforce the ideology of individualism that fuels their client's social exclusion in the first place" (2009, p. 339). That is to say that even in their attempts to contextualize their clients' homicidal behavior, defense attorneys will be forced to use individualizing language. To test this proposition, they analyzed the mitigation case presented in defense of "Daniel" in a southern state. The findings indicate that the helping agencies that were such a part of Daniel's early life—the welfare office, children's services, special education, mental healthcare, the juvenile justice system, and the like—relied upon individualizing psychological paradigms that decontextualized his problems and placed them inside of Daniel. According to the records, his problems are the result of individual pathology, not the social environment in which he exists: "Daniel's autonomous self is clearly identified as the problem. Nothing outside of Daniel needs to change; Daniel just needs to adjust. … Daniel is continually described as inherently and individually 'bad'" (Dunn and Kaplan, 2009, p. 354).

This type of record-keeping forced Daniel's defense attorneys to use individualizing language in their mitigation case: "Like other participants in both the law and the psy-complex, these attorneys locate the *source* of Daniel's problems within the borders of Daniel. Despite their good intentions of preventing Daniel's execution at the hands of the state, these attorneys perpetuate the psy-complex's project of profound individualization" (Dunn and Kaplan, 2009, p. 360). The individualistic nature of American culture and its legal system compels attorneys to use individualizing discourses that help instantiate and validate individualism. Individualistic accounts fill the defendants' records, and the law almost always expects individualized arguments. Individuals, not objective social conditions, are put on trial. Therefore, micro-level theories of human behavior are privileged to the exclusion of macro-level ones that illuminate the "sociocultural aspects of being human" (Dunn and Kaplan, 2009, p. 364). Unfortunately, Dunn and Kaplan's (2009) study is the only one that looks at the presentation of mitigating evidence in a capital case, so it is not known whether Daniel's case is typical, and there remains a giant hole in our understanding of capital mitigation. Do practitioners use other kinds of arguments? At this point, we simply do not know.

Capital Jurors and Individualism

Unlike the sentencing in most other cases, which is the exclusive province of judges, capital trials employ the use of lay-citizens in the sentencing process. Because of this reality, Haney (1997) has argued that commonsense understandings of crime and criminal behavior matter more in death penalty cases than in any other. However, the cultural constructions that create these commonsense notions cause jurors to defer to micro-level individualistic theories that suggest that homicidal violence "is carried out by dehumanized, anonymous figures or monsters rather than real people" who live in a social world and are affected by their environment (Haney, 2003, pp. 470-71). According to Haney (2003), the individualistic biases these jurors bring with them to capital trials and the lack of comprehension inherent in legalistic sentencing instructions combine to leave jurors unaware of why most mitigating evidence is even relevant, and there is a substantial amount of empirical evidence to support this conclusion.

In 1990, the Capital Jury Project (CJP) was launched in 14 states. With the principal objectives of examining capital jurors' use of sentencing discretion, identifying the extent and sources of arbitrariness in their decisions, and evaluating the ability of different capital sentencing statutes to alleviate arbitrariness (Bowers, 1995), the CJP collected data from 1,198 jurors who served on 353 different trials (Bowers et al., 2003). Using both open- and closed-ended responses in order to get both a depth and breadth of responses that could demonstrate the decision-making process of capital jurors and juries, the dynamics of jury interaction, the experiences of capital jurors, and their use of discretion, the CJP has shed significant light on the ways in which capital jurors make their sentencing decisions, and the findings offer strong support to the arguments made by Haney (2003) and to Dunn and Kaplan's (2009) theory of hegemonic individualism. Unfortunately, there is much less empirical examination of how the factors capital jurors identify as important in their sentencing decisions compare to the evidence *actually presented* at trial.

The CJP revealed that capital jurors are inclined to discount the relevance of mitigating evidence (Garvey, 1998; Sandys and McClelland, 2003) to the point where many could "accurately be described as mitigation deniers" (Sandys and McClelland, 2003, p. 405). For example, the central question for jurors from a case in Georgia was the defendant's culpability (Sarat, 1995). By insisting on the defendant's legal and moral culpability, the jurors refused "to accept the picture of a social world of events governed by causes beyond human control; instead, they constructed a moral world of free agents making choices for which they should be held to account" (Sarat, 1995, p. 1129). Across the entire sample, jurors were most likely to assign primary responsibility for the outcome of a capital trial to the defendant (Bowers et al., 2003; Hoffman, 1997), and they spent more time discussing the defendant's responsibility, the motive, and premeditation than they did discussing the defendant's background or upbringing (Hoffman, 1997). As Bentele and Bowers (2001) discovered, jurors are often preoccupied with evidence of guilt during punishment deliberations, believe that aggravating circumstances mandate (rather than permit) a death sentence, and fail to consider mitigating evidence. All of this suggests that jurors believe in the idea of individual responsibility.

The CJP also revealed the tendency of jurors to make their punishment decisions prior to the start of the penalty phase, which means they relied entirely on the individualized guilt-phase evidence and made their decisions prior to the defendant's ability to present mitigating evidence. Nearly half of the jurors interviewed had made a decision as to punishment prior to the start of the penalty trial (Bowers et al., 1998). Unsurprisingly, those jurors who prematurely decided on death were the least likely to consider mitigation (Brewer, 2004). Premature deciders admitted that they made their guilt and punishment decisions on the basis of the same evidence (Bowers et al., 2003), which suggests that context is not relevant to many (if not most) capital jurors. In fact, many early pro-death jurors said the reason for their early stance was proof of guilt or the nature of the crime (Bowers et al., 2003), which indicates they were completely uninterested in and closed off to contextualizing mitigation that had no direct nexus to the crime. In other words, these findings suggest that many capital jurors enter the courtroom predisposed to believe micro-level theories of human behavior that are predominantly focused on individual responsibility and are therefore unconcerned with anything other than who committed the crime and how heinous the crime was.

Many of these jurors also indicated that they viewed death as the "only acceptable" punishment, and many believed that certain aggravators, such as perceived future dangerousness or a "heinous, vile, or depraved" crime, mandated a death sentence (Bowers, 1996; Bowers et al., 2003). Such beliefs leave no room for the consideration of life history or context that might be relevant to understanding the crime. Although jurors are given instructions that tell them they are required to consider mitigating evidence, CJP interviews in North Carolina and South Carolina found that jurors did not understand these guidelines, which led them to improperly accept certain aggravators and reject mitigators (Bowers, 1996). Even when they do acknowledge the mitigation that has been presented, capital jurors do not necessarily abandon their decontextualized images of criminality. In California, it was found that capital jurors are often biased against defense experts because their testimonies do not comply with the jurors' understandings of human behavior or their own personal experiences, which causes the jurors to dismiss expert testimony as not credible or coming from a "hired gun" (Sundby, 1997). Many of the California capital jurors were able to identify others who experienced similar situations as the defendant did but turned out much differently as evidence that the mitigating circumstances were irrelevant. The defense experts' theories of human behavior are, therefore, typically discredited by jurors as invalid (Sundby, 1997). Indeed, "individual responsibility" is "a potent narrative" in the stories told by jurors who voted for death throughout the CJP sample (Fleury-Steiner, 2004). Much like the jurors interviewed by Sundby (1997) in California, Fleury-Steiner (2002; 2004) noted that jurors would take the idea that not everyone in a given circumstance ended up the same way as the defendant as evidence of the existence of individual choice and free will and of the irrelevance of social context.

Even when jurors do consider mitigation, they use an individualized lens to do so, focusing almost entirely on mitigating circumstances with a direct nexus to the criminal act. The most important mitigating circumstance identified by jurors is lingering doubt regarding the defendant's guilt, and the second most important one is evidence of mental retardation, which again focuses on the defendant's personal responsibility rather than social circumstances. Jurors were also willing to consider mental illness and extreme mental or emotional disturbance, which are again tied to the defendant's level of culpability (the guilt stage questions) or problems within the defendant (Garvey, 1998; Sandys and McClelland, 2003). Conversely, circumstances which may have contributed to the formation of a defendant's character (i.e., his/her social history) had a limited effect on jurors (Garvey, 1998). All of this research suggests that capital jurors are influenced by the hegemony of individualism. All that matters is the defendant's personal responsibility; the only mitigation that matters is that which directly reduces the defendant's culpability. Everything else is thought of as an excuse, rather than the explanation that it is.

The findings of these early CJP studies have been confirmed by other studies. Most pertinent is a study of capital jurors that was not conducted as part of the CJP. In this study, capital jurors from California and Oregon were interviewed, and it was determined that many capital jurors focused entirely on the nature of the crime during penalty deliberations and ignored background and context. Several of them even drew upon the idea that some people are able to overcome hardships in order to suggest that mitigating evidence was not relevant and that personal choice or free will is all that matters (Haney et al., 1994). Many of those interviewed even erroneously thought they were supposed to exclude any evidence not related directly to the execution of the crime while others dismissed presented mitigation because they did not understand that it was supposed to be considered as such (Haney, 1997). Many jurors even dismissed mitigating evidence altogether or actually re-interpreted it into aggravating evidence (Haney et al., 1994). Even studies using other samples confirm these overall findings. For example, a study of death-qualified jurors (not necessarily jurors who served on a capital trial) who were called to jury service in Cook County, Illinois, found that they do not understand the standard death sentencing instructions or grasp the purpose of mitigating evidence (Tiersma, 1995), and surveys of college students find that they too are more confused about the concept of mitigation than aggravation (Haney and Lynch, 1994; Haney and Lynch, 1997), suggesting that the influence of individualism is not limited to death-qualified capital jurors. Most of the students in these studies relied completely on the circumstances and nature of the crime in defining aggravation and mitigation, a move that ignores context and privileges aggravation over mitigation since aggravating circumstances are more likely to be related to the criminal act (Haney and Lynch, 1994; Haney and Lynch, 1997). Many potential mitigating factors were misunderstood by the subjects, the few that were understood related directly to the crime, the most inaccurately characterized factors were mitigators, and the least understood mitigator was the defendant's background and character, which also happens to be the one upon which defendants most often rely (Haney and Lynch, 1994; Haney and Lynch, 1997). In other words, even among a sample that is not death qualified and that is probably more liberal than the average capital juror, there is greater concern with the defendant's personal responsibility than the social context surrounding the crime.

Unfortunately, none of the studies using jurors who served on real trials used trial transcripts to discover whether defense attorneys even attempt to challenge individualism. Perhaps the jurors' individualistic answers were the result of highly individualized mitigating evidence—the kind presented in Dunn and Kaplan's (2009) study—that gave the jury little chance to consider context.

After all, recently published findings from Texas suggest that the arguments made by attorneys—especially prosecutors—during jury selection and the trial actually discourage jurors from considering mitigating evidence and may contribute to the jurors' disinclination to consider contextualizing evidence that bears no direct nexus to the crime (Vartkessian, 2011; Vartkessian, 2012). If this is true, it seems possible that evidence presented by the defense attorney may also impact what factors the jurors consider important in their sentencing decisions. Therefore, it is imperative to know what kinds of arguments capital jurors confront if we want to understand the role of hegemonic individualism in their sentencing decisions.

Judicial Decision Making

Although the numerous studies described above find ample evidence to suggest that most capital jurors do not understand the sentencing process and therefore fail to give the appropriate consideration to mitigating evidence, no study has yet looked at the decision making of judges in capital cases. However, there is some evidence to suggest that judges and jurors in non-capital contexts make decisions in very similar ways. In their classic study, *The American Jury*, Kalven and Zeisel (1966) found there was a 78 percent concordance rate between judges and juries in determining guilt, and this rate has remained virtually unchanged in the intervening years (Givelber and Farrell, 2012). Since that time, several studies have reached the conclusion that judges and jurors use similar decision-making processes in non-capital cases. Early experimental work found that regardless of whether it was deemed admissible, biasing evidence in civil cases had similar effects on judges and jurors (Landsman and Rakos, 1994). Similar to the jurors in CJP studies, judges also seem to favor individualizing information over statistical and background data (Guthrie et al., 2001). Even liberal-leaning judges discount the importance of life history by arguing that some people who experienced certain conditions did not turn out to be criminals (Haney, 1995), an argument that supports individualistic free will theories of behavior while trivializing potentially important mitigating circumstances. When judges and juries disagree on the verdict in non-capital criminal trials, it has been found that jurors are more receptive to the evidence presented by the defense, are more likely to acquit, and return verdicts that are less racially biased than judges (Givelber and Farrell, 2012), which suggests that judges may be even *less* receptive to mitigating evidence—especially contextual mitigation—than jurors.

However, capital mitigation is an exceedingly complex area of the law that contains a large body of case law and differs substantially from the factual decisions jurors are typically asked to make, so the findings discussed in the preceding paragraph may not be relevant for understanding how judges make decisions in capital cases. When the law is complex, there is evidence that judges do a better job than jurors of following the law. For example, judges are better able to set aside evidence obtained due to an illegal search or confession than laypersons are (Wistrich et al., 2005). Judges are (usually) lawyers. Because of their extensive legal training and experience, judges should have a better understanding of Supreme Court case law and the relevance and importance of mitigating evidence, thus they may be better placed to understand, interpret, and make use of mitigating evidence than lay-jurors. Yet, since no study has yet looked at the way judges in capital cases make their sentencing decisions, their receptivity to mitigation—especially mitigation derived from the environmental influences of the defendant's life history—remains an open question.

The Delaware Study

The existing literature leaves several questions unanswered. It remains entirely unclear what is happening on the ground in capital mitigation, how America's culture of retributive individualism impacts capital sentencing, or how the capital sentencing process—especially capital mitigation—can reproduce and substantiate individualism or challenge its basic tenets. How do defense attorneys frame the conduct of their clients? Are they using the opportunity provided by the mitigation process to tell contextualizing stories that are able to connect behavior to the impact of social forces, or are they focused on individualized questions such as culpability and mental capacity? Perhaps just as importantly, how do jurors and judges receive and understand mitigating evidence? Prior studies tell us that jurors are focused on individual responsibility, but is that because they have only been presented with individualizing arguments? How do they respond to truly contextualizing evidence, and how do they reach their sentencing recommendations? What evidence is most important to them? As for judges, there is no evidence as to how they make their sentencing decisions, but as judicial elites, they hold a special power to construct cultural master narratives. Therefore, it is crucial to understand how they make their sentencing decisions and the messages they convey to the public. Are they receptive to contextualizing evidence, or are they beholden to hegemonic individualism? How do they use (or misuse or ignore) mitigation? On what evidence do they base their sentencing decisions, and, most importantly, what messages about human behavior are they creating in their sentencing opinions? Do they perpetuate or challenge individualistic mentalities?

In order to explore and offer a preliminary answer to these questions, this study performs an in-depth qualitative analysis of eight mitigation cases in Delaware. In this way it builds on the work of Dunn and Kaplan (2009) by conducting an analysis of multiple mitigation cases—half of which were successful—but it also goes a step further to investigate how decision makers respond to different mitigation strategies. A qualitative approach was chosen because the mitigation process can only be fully understood with a detailed narrative analysis that is able to give attention to detailed descriptions. Because the effective presentation of mitigating evidence requires the defense team to bring the defendant's story to life, it is often rich and multidimensional (American Bar Association, 2003;

American Bar Association, 2008; Bruno, 2010; Cheng, 2010; Freedman, 2008; Holdman and Seeds, 2008). As such, mitigating stories need to be understood with attention to both consistent patterns and to details that may appear idiosyncratic but that are actually critical for achieving a fuller understanding (Riessman, 1993). Developing an in-depth picture of mitigation narratives requires a "detailed, intensive, microscopic examination of the data in order to bring out the amazing complexity of what lies in, behind, and beyond those data" (Strauss, 1987, p. 10). It also requires a detailed narrative analysis of both the content that is presented in mitigation cases *and* how that evidence is received, understood, processed, and utilized by decision makers. This type of analysis is best conducted qualitatively because an in-depth qualitative study can provide insights and details into the nature of how mitigating evidence is presented and used that a larger quantitative study cannot.

Although a qualitative study of eight cases is clearly incapable of being generalized, the goal of this study is not to generalize. While this study could potentially reveal problems in the implementation of the death sentence that require further empirical investigations that are generalizeable, the goal of this work is to expand on the work of Dunn and Kaplan (2009) by providing an exploratory analysis of the cultural and institutional life of capital mitigation and providing a preliminary answer to the dual questions of how cultural discourse impacts the mitigation process and how that mitigation process, in turn, helps to construct cultural narratives. Therefore, generalizeability is not an overriding concern; although, it is hoped that this study can provide the framework for future explanatory analyses.

Sampling

Because generalizeability was not a major concern, the sample for this project was not randomly selected. Eight capital trials that concluded (i.e., the sentence was pronounced) during the years 2001-2005 and included both a guilt and a sentencing phase were selected based upon convenience. The reason this time period was chosen was to maximize both the number of available cases and juror recall. Data were collected between March 2009 and December 2010. It was feared that cases that concluded prior to 2001 would cause jurors' memories to be too faded but that cases that concluded after 2005 might still be under state appellate review and therefore not have transcripts or sentencing opinions available. During the sampling time period, there were 11 death sentences issued in Delaware, but three of these were overturned on appeal and were therefore excluded. A fourth defendant refused to allow his attorney to present any mitigating factors, so his case was also excluded (since this is a study of mitigation). Because acquiring trial transcripts through the court reporter in Delaware is cost prohibitive ($2 per page and penalty trials are often more than 1000 pages long), I had to rely on transcripts available through other sources. Of the remaining seven death cases, four had electronic copies of their transcripts available at no cost from the Philadelphia

Federal Defenders Office, and so they were selected for inclusion. There were 14 life sentences issued following a capital penalty trial held before a jury during these five years;[1] however, two of these cases had to be dropped. In the first, the jury failed to unanimously find the existence of at least one statutory aggravating circumstance and so the defendant was no longer death eligible and sentencing was removed from the judge's hands. In the second, the defendant was a juvenile when the crime was committed and *Roper v. Simmons* (2005), which bars the execution of juvenile offenders, was decided between the conclusion of the penalty hearing and the judge's determination of sentence. Because double-jeopardy protections prevent life sentences from being appealed, most life cases in Delaware do not have penalty phase transcripts readily available. By contacting appellate attorneys and coding transcripts that existed in the court files, I was able to acquire data from four life cases during this period. Because I wanted to examine the differences in the presentation of mitigation and the receptivity of sentencers to mitigation in life and death cases and since the ratio of death sentences to life sentences in Delaware capital cases since 1991 (when the current death sentencing procedure was enacted) is nearly one-to-one (Fleury-Steiner et al., 2009, p. 18),[2] I wanted an equal number of life and death cases. Therefore, the sample consists of four life and four death cases.

Within this sample, jurors were selected systematically. The interview data with the capital jurors was collected as part of the third phase of the Capital Jury Project (CJP3). The goal of the CJP3 was to sample six jurors from each trial. To be included in the sample jurors had to serve on *both* the guilt and the punishment phase of the trial; this excluded two jurors who did not serve on both trials, reducing the sampling frame to 94 jurors. Those jurors were then arranged alphabetically by first name within their respective juries and assigned a number (one through 12) with each odd numbered juror being included in the sample. Of course, not every juror who was sampled could be interviewed. Many could not be located because they did not have a listed telephone number or address, some had moved away, others did not return repeated phone calls or declined to participate, and a few, unfortunately, had passed away. If an odd-numbered juror could not be interviewed, he or she was replaced with the next even-numbered juror in line. If that juror could also not be interviewed, the next even-numbered juror was included. This process was repeated until either the sampling goal of six jurors was met or the list of jurors was exhausted. Using this method, 35 of the

1 It should be noted that there were other life sentences in non-capital first degree murder cases and there were two defendants sentenced to life following a penalty hearing held without a jury. In this case, there was also no guilt trial; the penalty hearing was the result of the defendants' earlier death sentences being overturned by the Delaware Supreme Court.

2 According to the author's own records, between the date of the law change and the end of 2011, there were 40 offenders sentenced to death and, excluding the case of the juvenile, there were 41 defendants sentenced to life following a capital penalty trial.

intended 48 jurors were located and interviewed (72.9 percent of the goal). The jurors were also compensated for their time. As will be described below, Delaware capital juries only make a non-binding recommendation on sentence in capital cases that does not need to be unanimous. Therefore, there are jurors who voted for a different sentence who served on the same case. There were 13 jurors from the four death cases (all of whom voted for death) and 22 jurors from the four life cases (half of whom voted for death). Although the overrepresentation of jurors from life cases is a little concerning, since this is a study of mitigation and mitigation is presumably stronger in life cases, this concern is not overpowering. In fact, jurors from life cases may be more informative when it comes to understanding how mitigation works. Within the sample, there were 18 males and 17 females. Overall in these eight cases, 56.3 percent of the jurors voted for death,[3] compared to 68.6 percent in the sample, and 47.9 percent of the jurors were male, compared to 51.4 percent in the sample.

Table 1.1 Breakdown of jurors by case by vote and gender

Defendant	Sample (*n*=35)				Sampling Frame (*n*=94)			
	Death Votes	Life Votes	Males	Females	Death Votes	Life Votes	Males	Females
Donald (L)	3	3	2	4	5	7	4	8
Ted (L)	2	4	2	4	3	9	5	7
Roger (L)	5	1	3	3	5	7	5	6
Alan (L)	1	3	2	2	1	11	4	7
Charlie (D)	2	0	2	0	12	0	5	7
Michael (D)	3	0	2	1	7	5	6	6
Steve (D)	3	0	2	1	9	3	9	3
Jerry (D)	5	0	3	2	12	0	7	5
Total	**24**	**11**	**18**	**17**	**54**	**42**	**45**	**49**

Note: One juror from Donald's case reported that she did not serve on the penalty phase despite records to the contrary. I believe based on her other responses that she probably voted for life, so I coded her as a "life" juror. The male/female count for the sampling frame is based upon the names on the jury list; it is possible some jurors got miscoded if they had an androgynous name. Because it is not known how the two jurors who were excluded because they did not serve on the guilt trial voted, their votes could not be excluded so there are 96 votes in the sampling frame.

3 It is not known how the two jurors who were excluded because they did not serve on the guilt phase voted, so this number is based on the total vote count of all 96 jurors who recommended a sentence in these eight trials.

Methodology

To begin the analysis, the transcripts were open coded for the reasons defense teams gave for why their clients should not be executed. This method revealed four predominant themes that will be discussed in greater detail in subsequent chapters: lack of culpability, the impact of an execution on the defendant's family and friends, the ability of life without parole (LWOP) to achieve the same goals as a death sentence, and the defendant's upbringing and background. Each mitigating argument made by the defense attorneys and mitigation experts was then coded for whether it individualized the defendant's behavior (that is, focused on micro-level causal forces within the defendant like his free will or psychological problems) or contextualized it (that is, focused on macro-level external causal forces such as abuse, poverty, or the subculture of violence). In other words, does each mitigating argument challenge or reinforce hegemonic individualism?

Next, the juror interviews were analyzed. The jurors were interviewed using a standardized 53-page, 138-question interview guide provided by the CJP3. The questions have been reproduced in the Appendix. The primary goal of the CJP3 was to assess jurors' receptivity to mitigation. The questionnaire asks jurors about their recall of specific witnesses during the trial and what they remember about those witnesses. It also probes the jurors' receptivity to mitigation by asking them how certain testimony was received and how it affected their sentencing recommendations. This allows for a comparison to what really happened and enables interviewers to ask about and remind jurors about specific testimony. These questions get to the heart of jurors' receptivity to mitigating evidence by gauging how influential certain testimony was and allowing jurors' responses to be linked with the actual mitigating evidence presented by the defense. The interviews typically lasted slightly more than three hours; although they were as short as two-and-a-half and as long as four-and-a-half hours. Thirty-one of the interviews were conducted face-to-face, one was conducted half over the phone and half in person, and three others were conducted over the phone. Twenty-nine of the interviews were completed in a single session, but due to time constraints, six had to be conducted over multiple meetings.

Although the entire interview transcription was analyzed for all 35 jurors, special attention was paid to the sections that asked the jurors their reasons for voting as they did, which evidence they found most influential, which penalty trial witnesses and testimony they recalled, and what they thought about the testimony of each witness. The jurors' responses were coded for whether they used individualistic (i.e., dispositional, rational choice, free will, micro-level) or environmental (i.e., situational, contextual, macro-level) explanations for the defendants' behavior, and then, for each juror, the mitigating evidence identified in the trial transcripts was coded for whether the juror ignored/forgot it, remembered it but did not consider it relevant, remembered it but was hostile to it, or was less likely to vote for death because of it. In order to ensure the confidentiality of all jurors, pseudonyms will be used to refer to the defendants and the jurors.

Lastly, the written sentencing opinions of the trial judges in all eight cases were read, coded, and analyzed. Five different Superior Court judges, all of whom are white males, presided over these eight trials. None of the judges served on more than two of the cases in the sample. As with the juror interviews, each judicial opinion was coded for whether it offered a contextual or individualistic explanation for the defendant's behavior. Each passage of the opinions that focused on the defendant's behavior was coded for whether it located the cause of that behavior within the defendant or outside the defendant, and the opinions were also coded for whether they offered an overall message that supported or subverted hegemonic individualism. That is, what was the judge's overall rationale for choosing the sentence he chose? Lastly, the mitigating arguments identified in the trial transcripts were coded for whether the judges considered them strongly mitigating, moderately mitigating, slightly mitigating, or aggravating, whether they ignored it altogether, or mentioned it but did not factor it into their decisions. Although the sentencing opinions are public records, the goal of this study is not to challenge or criticize any judge. Therefore, judges will not be referenced by name, a practice that should also help to protect the confidentiality of the jurors.

Why Delaware?

It might be objected that this study only uses one state and therefore cannot be generalized nor answer broad questions about American culture or sentencing policy. While this may be true, this study is designed as an exploratory one, a starting point for future inquiries into the mitigation process. In order to do this, an intensive multi-source analysis is necessary. For one thing, because most of the laws under which Americans live are enacted at the local and state levels, different states have different ways of determining punishment in murder cases. According to Barker, "Individual states tend to punish differently from one another and punish in ways that have not been fully documented, understood, and explained" (2009, p. 4). Since this variation is especially pronounced in the use of the death penalty, a state-level analysis is important for gaining a more nuanced understanding. Considering the differences in laws regarding the determination of sentence in capital cases and the differences in the way jurors are instructed to consider mitigation, if multiple states were to be included, it would make comparison of cases across state lines impossible, which would destroy the value of a multi-case, multi-source study.

While studies of national trends are clearly important, and it is hoped that this study can provide the framework for future (generalizeable) national studies of individualism and mitigation, "The reality of American penal sanctioning is much more complicated, uneven, and obscure than the discussion of national trends allows" (Barker, 2009, p. 6). Decisions about how and why to punish are intimately tied to historical, cultural, political, and social contexts and processes (Barker, 2009; Garland, 1990; Garland, 2001). Substantial variations in punishment practices and trends may well be the result of subtle differences along these dimensions among various states. More detailed and nuanced sub-national studies are thus required for a fuller understanding of American penal practices. For this reason, this study is an in-depth analysis of a single state.

So, why was Delaware, a relatively small state chosen for this project? Delaware was chosen for a variety of strategic reasons. The most important reason was that Delaware is one of only three states that utilizes a hybrid capital sentencing scheme in which jurors are relegated to an advisory role during sentencing and final sentencing authority in capital cases is vested in judges, who are *required* to file a written sentencing opinion in *every* capital case (11 Del. C. §4209(d)(4)). This unique setup allows trial judges to come to the forefront of empirical examination. As described above, it is not known how judges act in these circumstances and there is evidence to suggest they might be less receptive to mitigation and evidence to suggest the opposite. The truth is, we just do not know. However, as judicial elites, judges have the power to frame crime stories and create cultural master narratives about homicidal violence in a way that few others do. Therefore, their stories are critically important to understanding the reciprocal effects of law and society. Furthermore, judges in Delaware are appointed to 12-year terms (the longest in the United States) by the governor through a merit selection process and do not face retention elections (American Judicature Society, 2012; Delaware State Courts, n.d.). The other two states using hybrid death sentencing laws (Florida and Alabama) both select their judges using popular elections (American Judicature Society, 2012). This should insulate the Delaware judges from the whims of public opinion and the fear of angering their voters, thus freeing them to consider mitigating evidence in the way the Supreme Court intended. After all, judges who face elections are more sensitive to popular opinion (Pinello, 1995), particularly in capital cases (Brace and Boyea, 2007; Brooks and Raphael, 2003). Therefore, of all actors in the criminal justice system, Delaware judges should be in the best position to consider contextual mitigation and offer a challenge to hegemonic individualism.

Another aspect of Delaware that makes it appealing as a research site is that it is a border state that is politically and socially heterogeneous. Northern Delaware is more urbanized, resembles its Mid-Atlantic neighbors, and is politically liberal whereas Southern Delaware is rural and sparsely populated, resembles South Atlantic states, and is politically conservative. In a way, therefore, Delaware actually possesses features that allow it to resemble both northern and southern states and to act as a microcosm of the United States as a whole. This heterogeneity makes it an interesting location for studying the relationship between culture and the law—especially the culture of individualism, which has been linked to conservative public policies (Beckett, 1997; Beckett and Sasson, 2000; Brake and Hale, 1992).

Delaware is also an appealing research location because there is little known about how its death penalty operates. Delaware has been mostly overlooked by death penalty scholars despite the fact that it has the third highest death sentence-to-murder ratio in America (Blume et al., 2004), at one point it had the highest per capita execution rate in the United States (Fleury-Steiner et al., 2009, p. 18), and it exhibits more race-based sentencing disparity than any other jurisdiction (Johnson et al., 2012). These numbers actually reflect a punitive death sentencing history that makes Delaware an intriguing location to research the law's relationship to hegemonic individualism. Unlike Florida and Alabama, which developed their hybrid sentencing schemes following the Supreme Court's decision in *Furman v. Georgia* (1972), Delaware came to its statute quite deliberately following the high profile murders of two white armored car guards by four black men from Philadelphia. After its mandatory death penalty was invalidated by the Supreme Court's decision in *Woodson v. North Carolina* (1976), Delaware adopted the system used in most states that requires a jury to unanimously determine sentence. However, in 1991, two days after the jury failed to sentence the four men convicted of killing the two armored car guards to death (one juror held out for a life sentence), the state legislature radically altered the death penalty statute to relegate the jury to an advisory role (Fleury-Steiner et al., 2009), which caused the number of death sentences to skyrocket (Johnson, et al., 2012). The narratives used by the media and legislators in pushing for this law change reflected a highly individualistic worldview in which there is "a stark dichotomy between 'good' and 'bad' people" (Fleury-Steiner et al., 2009, p. 11).

Twelve years later, the legislature again radically altered the state's death sentencing statute, this time in response to a decision by the state Supreme Court. In 2003, the Delaware Supreme Court overturned the death sentence of Sadiki Garden because the judge sentenced Garden to death despite a 9-3 jury recommendation for life. The Court reasoned that unless no reasonable person could agree with a life sentence, the judge must give the jury's recommendation "great weight," which in effect made life recommendations binding on trial judges (*Garden v. State*, 2003). Five months later, a bill was introduced into the Delaware House of Representatives with the express purpose of overturning the Supreme Court's decision (Spence, 2003). The bill, which passed the House the very same day it was introduced and was signed into law less than three weeks later, specified that although the judge must consider a jury's recommendation, "he or she shall not be bound by the recommendation, but instead shall give it such weight as he or she deems appropriate" (Spence, 2003). The existing language of the state's capital sentencing statute states that jury recommendations "shall not be binding upon the Court" and that the recommendations "shall be given such consideration as deemed appropriate by the Court" (Del. C., Title 11, §4209(d)(1)), which in effect gives judges in Delaware more freedom to decide sentence than judges in either Florida or Alabama.

Lastly, Delaware is a timely research location. In March 2013, the Delaware Senate voted to repeal the death penalty (Rini, 2013a). Although the state's House of Representatives never brought the bill to a full vote, supporters of repeal have vowed to continue fighting (Rini, 2013b). Therefore, a book that offers an in-depth exploration of the operation of the state's death penalty can help inform a current policy debate and potentially influence the outcome of this debate. It is with this hope in mind that I proceed to discuss the findings of this study.

Chapter 2
Hegemonic Tales of Individual Responsibility in Capital Mitigation

> "But [defendant], as you will remember, and I know that you will, was charged with not an intentional killing, not a reckless killing, but with negligently causing the death during the commission of a robbery."

> "If you feel that he wasn't the actual killer, that if you feel he was involved, but more as an accomplice, we hope that it will have an impact on you ..."

> "As a result of your verdict ... you've already imposed a death sentence on [defendant]. Because of that verdict, [defendant] is going to die in jail."

The trial transcripts reveal that what is happening on the ground in capital mitigation may be more complex and nuanced than Dunn and Kaplan (2009) had envisioned. Rather than being focused exclusively on individualizing factors, there were actually four predominant mitigation arguments that emerged from the transcripts: the defendant's lack of culpability, the ability of a life sentence to achieve the same goals (i.e., incapacitation, retribution, deterrence) as a death sentence, the defendant's life history, and the defendant's basic humanity. However, the first two lines of reasoning are both micro-level in nature and they both support and reinforce the hegemonic narrative of individual responsibility in the ways Dunn and Kaplan (2009) feared. These arguments were used by the defense in *all eight* trials in this sample, which indicates that Dunn and Kaplan were at least partially right to fear that the efforts of defense attorneys to save their clients' lives may "perpetuate the psy-complex's project of profound individualization" and cause defense attorneys to win "one death penalty case while losing a more sustained battle against the ideology of individualism that fuels their client's social exclusion" (2009, p. 360). In fact, the "lack of culpability" argument explicitly adopts the psy-complex's view of individual responsibility and causes attorneys to "draw upon individuating discourses that frame the defendant as responsible" (Dunn and Kaplan, 2009, p. 338).

These findings reveal the true power of hegemonic tales: they compel even those who may oppose them to adapt their own stories to fit within the hegemonic narrative. Even if they wanted to challenge hegemonic individualism, the attorneys were unable to offer a full frontal assault. As suggested by the literature discussed in Chapter 1, and as revealed in the findings in Chapters 4 and 5, the ways in which jurors and judges make decisions forces attorneys to draw upon commonsense notions of responsibility attribution if they are going to have any chance of saving their clients' lives. These are the types of arguments that are likely to be effective with these decision makers who enter the courtroom with biases toward micro-level theories and who are exposed to the individualistic question of guilt prior to sitting through the penalty trial. Attorneys who only offer stories that challenge hegemonic individualism may actually be placing their own clients in greater peril because they offer stories that do not register with jurors' and judges' taken-for-granted assumptions about human behavior. Therefore, the power of hegemonic individualism actually places defense attorneys in the unenviable position of being forced to support the very individualism that supports capital punishment in the first place.

"Not an Intentional Killing": Culpability and Individualism in Capital Mitigation

Because of the premium placed on individual responsibility in American culture, trying to diminish the defendant's culpability in an individualistic manner may be one of the best strategic moves a defense attorney can make, and so all eight defense teams tried to cast doubt as to the defendant's state of mind. They either suggested that an accomplice was more blameworthy, that the killing was unintentional, or that the defendant experienced mental limitations that diminished his culpability.

"He Wasn't the Actual Killer"

If there was more than one perpetrator involved in the crime, defense attorneys took this opportunity to attempt to cast doubt as to the identity of the true killer and to portray the accomplice or accomplices as more blameworthy than the defendant. The mitigation case presented in defense of Alan[1] offers a case-in-point. Alan and a co-defendant were originally tried together for the attempted robbery and murder of a local vendor, but after the jury was hung, they were re-tried separately. The evidence indicated both defendants had a gun during the robbery attempt but that they fled without any money after both of their guns discharged; it was not clear which gun fired the fatal bullet or even if the shot was fired intentionally. In his re-trial, Alan was convicted of murder after nearly three days of jury deliberations. Hypothesizing that the length of deliberations might suggest that there were some lingering doubts as to Alan's role in the killing, the defense team used both their

1 In order to help protect the confidentiality of the jurors, all crime descriptions are generic and all defendants are identified with a pseudonym. Due to the small size of Delaware and its small absolute number of capital cases, providing too many details would risk betraying jurors' identities. The four death cases in this sample, for example, encompass half of those who were sentenced to death and did not have their sentence overturned during the time period of this study.

opening and closing statements to suggest Alan might not be culpable enough to receive a death sentence. In his opening statement, Alan's attorney asked, "What was the defendant's involvement? Apply it to what you thought about for the last—for three days, what you argued about, what you talked about. What was his role?" Alan's defense team even called an attorney to the stand to explain the idea of accomplice liability to the jurors, presumably to remind them that just because they convicted the defendant does not mean they decided he was the trigger-man, and then in their summation, they implored the jurors to consider the State's evidence in the guilt phase and to decide that Alan did not shoot the victim: "But in deciding whether to recommend life, you can consider … all the evidence in this case. Two and a half days of discussions, two and a half days reviewing the evidence, something in those [guilt] discussions may suggest to you that life is the more appropriate sentence."

Donald's penalty defense also utilized doubts as to the killer's identity. Donald was convicted of felony murder in the robbery and killing of a clerk, but he was acquitted of intentional murder as it was unclear what his role in the crime was. Two co-conspirators fingered the defendant as the shooter, but video surveillance could not definitely identify the shooter. At trial, the defense argued that one of the co-perpetrators was the trigger-man, and they maintained this line of attack in the penalty phase. In his opening statement, Donald's defense attorney argued:

> We hope that you've spoken volumes about the role you feel [Donald] played in this homicide. We hope that that will have, because it should, an impact on your recommendation during the penalty phase; that is, that if you feel that he wasn't the actual killer, that if you feel he was involved, but more as an accomplice, we hope that it will have an impact on you to know that you sit in judgment over whether he dies or not because he was an accomplice and the actual killers will ultimately get out of jail, or he lives the rest of his life in jail.

In the closing arguments, the defense again stressed Donald's role, telling the jury that if they believed the defendant was the getaway driver rather than the actual killer, this should be a mitigator and that if they had "reasonable doubt that he was a major participant" that he should be spared, especially when compared to the fact "that the actual killer pled guilty to robbery and firearm offenses and will be released someday."

Roger's defense team also tried to deflect guilt from their client by focusing on co-perpetrators. At the guilt trial, Roger was convicted of contacting an acquaintance under the guise of making a bootlegged music purchase and then robbing him. In an effort to prevent being implicated in the robbery, he shot the victim several times in the back, killing him. Although Roger got a ride to the victim's house by a friend, the prosecution never alleged that this friend was aware of the plan to rob or kill the victim. Nevertheless, the defense argued in their opening that two other persons were involved in the crime, that the murder was committed with a gun owned by one of these alleged accomplices and found in the house of the other, and that one of the accomplices knew the victim and drove the defendant on the date of the offense. The defense then asked the jury if they thought it was "fair that those two guys go almost virtually scot-free and [Roger] takes the heat for all that." In the summation, the same rationale was presented: "Please consider the lack of fairness of sentencing [Roger] to death when [alleged accomplice] serves not a single day for his role as an accomplice in the murder of [victim]."

In Michael's case, Michael and a co-perpetrator were convicted of breaking into a house and killing a young father and husband in a home-invasion robbery, but the evidence could not determine which offender fired the fatal bullet. Utilizing this doubt, the defense asked the jury to consider the role Michael played, and during closing arguments, they argued that the co-perpetrator had the gun and shot the victim. He even suggested that if the jurors had any "residual doubt" over the defendant's involvement that they should consider that a mitigating circumstance.

Steve was convicted of participating in a double-murder in which one victim was severely beaten before both victims were shot execution-style in the back of the head. The evidence suggested that the co-defendant, who was older, was the driving force behind the murders, but no evidence established who fired the fatal shots. Once again, the defense attorneys attempted to capitalize on this doubt by suggesting the accomplice was the more culpable party. As Steve's attorney put it in his opening statement,

> There is another issue we are going to ask you to consider in this penalty phase and that concerns [Steve's] roles in these crimes. Your verdict did not indicate whether you found him guilty as a principal or accomplice. The evidence tended to show that only one gun was used, one triggerman. We will ask you to consider during this hearing whether you can feel comfortable voting to execute someone, a teenage accomplice, who maybe you felt did not pull the trigger …

In the closing argument, Steve's defense repeated this theme. The attorney suggested that the crime was probably the co-perpetrator's idea and that the co-perpetrator probably pulled the trigger. He said the State did not prove who pulled the trigger and argued, "You are being asked to execute someone who probably did not pull the trigger, who probably did not come up with this murderous idea, who probably would not have been involved in this case were it not for [co-perpetrator]." He then asked the jurors if they felt the defendant should "get the same sentence as the man who had the idea, as the man who roped him into the plan …"

"Not an Intentional Killing"

Another common individualizing tactic used by defense attorneys, especially those who could not point to possible co-conspirators, was to turn to the defendant's state of mind to suggest that the defendant did not deserve death or that no statutory aggravators existed. Ted's case offers a great example of this strategy. Ted was convicted of negligently killing another man during a botched robbery. Two co-conspirators lured the victim and a friend into an ambush in which Ted planned to rob both men at gunpoint. Unfortunately, one of the men resisted and was fatally shot in the torso during the ensuing struggle; the other victim was chased down and beaten but allowed to live. In his summation, Ted's attorney argued:

> But [Ted], as you will remember, and I know that you will, was charged with not an intentional killing, not a reckless killing, but with negligently causing the death during the commission of a robbery.
>
> If [Ted] were the danger[ous], cold, calculating killer that is so feared, why let [surviving robbery victim] go?
>
> [Prosecutor] talked about [surviving robbery victim]'s testimony, talked about what he said happened to him. He was not killed. There is no evidence that [Ted] intended to kill anyone …

This strategy was not restricted to felony murders or cases in which there was some doubt over the defendant's intent to kill. Even when the killer's intention to kill was clear, the defense team argued that the killer lacked sufficient premeditation to warrant a death sentence. For example, Charlie was convicted of a particularly newsworthy double murder in which a young child was killed by a stray bullet. Noticing a man with whom he had previous altercations, Charlie got out of the car in which he was riding, put a mask over his face, pursued his victim into a local business, and opened fire on his victim. In the hail of gunfire, both Charlie's intended victim, who tried to flee, and a young child were killed; the child died in his father's arms. Charlie's lawyers tried to use the fact that Charlie was not aiming for the child as a mitigator: "There's never been a suggestion that this execution-style shooting was targeted at [child victim]. … That was not what was intended when this whole thing started." They reiterated this argument in the closing: "… under no circumstances was there ever any preplanned or premeditated intention to kill [child victim]. This case is different from the case of an individual who plans and premeditates and kills …"

Jerry's defense team used a similar strategy in an attempt to challenge the prosecution's alleged statutory aggravating circumstances. Jerry was convicted of killing his wife by shooting her in the head. The prosecution alleged that he killed her to collect an insurance policy on her life and to move in with his mistress, so they presented two statutory aggravators: "The murder was committed for pecuniary gain" (11 Del. C. §4209(e)(1)o), and "The murder was premeditated and the result of substantial planning" (11 Del. C. §4209(e)(1)u). The defense tried to refute these claims by arguing, "All the testimony and all the evidence go to the actions of [Jerry] after [victim]'s death." Throughout the mitigation case, they tried to suggest that even though Jerry was guilty of this murder, the crime was impulsive rather than calculated; if he had a plan, it was a plan to cover up the murder that was not formed until after the victim was already dead. He was not a cold-blooded killer with a plan or a desire to cash in an insurance policy; rather, he killed the victim in the heat of the moment and then tried to cover it up (poorly) after the fact. They even talked about how bad Jerry's attempt to cover up the crime was in an attempt to show that he did not plan the killing in advance.

"You Tend to Be Born With This"

A final method attorneys used in their efforts to divest their clients of responsibility for the crimes of which they were convicted was to discuss mental limitations that originated inside their clients. The psychiatrist in Charlie's trial discussed Charlie's chronic depression, learning disorder, and borderline intellectual functioning, which impaired his judgment, analytical ability, and ability to process information. In the defense's closing argument, the judge and jury were reminded that the defendant "was cognitively deficient" and "experienced depression." In two other cases, a psychologist testified as to the defendant's mental impairments. In Steve's case, a psychologist testified that the defendant had an impulsive personality and a history of ADHD that made it harder for him to think his actions through. In Ted's trial, a psychologist testified that the defendant was bipolar and had ADHD, which led to inattentiveness and impulse control problems. In his direct testimony, the psychologist opined, "But there are serious mental-health problems which interferes [*sic*] with this man's ability to function at all times." In describing the problems, he explained that "you tend to be born with this. We don't know why. It seems to be a genetic link. ... It's got to do with some wiring that's not the same as the normal person." The defendant's problems here were described as internal and uncontrollable. Because of this, the problem "doesn't go away. You don't outgrow it. ... you're stuck with it," according to the expert.

These factors are certainly mitigating in nature and should be presented to a jury for consideration, but they do not contextualize the defendants' decisions. This testimony was designed to suggest that the defendants were less culpable because their brains did not work properly. This is the same strategy Dunn and Kaplan discovered "Daniel's" attorneys were using: "Daniel ... is less morally culpable than 'normal people' because he carries 'problems'—neurological impairments and emotional disturbance—within his person" (2009, p. 360) The focus in both Dunn and Kaplan's (2009) example and the Delaware cases analyzed here was on individual responsibility. The defendants were less culpable because of an internal problem rather than external influences. In his summation, the defense attorney in Ted's trial even went as far to say "that ADHD is not just caused by your environment. There's an actual brain defect." In other words, he was telling jurors they could consider this mitigating circumstance because it was a problem that originated within the defendant.

"The Only Way He'll Leave Prison Will Be in a Coffin"

Another individualizing argument presented by the defense in *all eight* trials was to stress that the alternative penalty in Delaware is life without parole (LWOP), which means a true life sentence. This line of reasoning basically involved two steps: trying to convince the jurors that they do not need to worry about the defendant ever getting out of prison because those sentenced to LWOP really do die in prison, and then trying to convince them that LWOP could accomplish the same sentencing goals as death. This was probably a smart strategy on the part of the defense lawyers because capital jurors tend to underestimate how long capital murderers who are not sentenced to death stay in prison, those who underestimate the alternative penalty are more likely to support a death sentence, and many jurors who vote for a death sentence do not actually want the defendant executed—they just believe that a death sentence is the only way to achieve a LWOP sentence (Bowers and Steiner, 1999). By reminding jurors that in Delaware life really does mean life, attorneys were probably trying to convince these "death to ensure LWOP" jurors that they could achieve LWOP with a life sentence.

Although this is probably a good strategy on the part of defense attorneys, it is still an individualizing argument because it does not focus on any background factors that may explain the defendant's conduct, nor does it place the defendant within a social milieu that may have affected his behavior. Instead of discussing how altering the environment could impact the defendant's actions, this line of reasoning focuses solely on the defendant as an agent of violence who deserves punishment. It just takes the viewpoint that LWOP is sufficient to protect the public from the defendant and that he will suffer enough in prison. The attorneys seem to be telling the jurors that it was okay to give the defendant a life sentence because this is a sufficiently harsh penalty that could still protect the community and that the jurors were not being soft on crime by sparing the defendant's life.

The "life means life" argument was never the primary focus of any mitigation case, and experts were not typically called explicitly to discuss the topic. Rather, the attorneys appeared to just throw the argument into their opening and closing statements, probably to assuage the fears of jurors that the defendant may be released someday. However, on occasion a defense expert would opine that prison would be sufficient to prevent a defendant from committing future acts of violence. Combined with the arguments made by the attorneys, this testimony helped to convey the point that LWOP had an equally retributive and incapacitating capability as death, but it also indirectly lent support to these two individualistic sentencing rationales by suggesting that they should be the rationales we use to determine punishment.

Life Equals Death

The first step in this process was to try equating a life sentence with a death sentence to convince the jurors that a life sentence actually does entail the defendant staying in prison until he dies. If the outcome of both sentences is the same, then the jury can accomplish the same goals with a life sentence but without having to get blood on their hands. At a minimum every single defense team mentioned in both their opening statement and closing argument that the alternative penalty in Delaware is LWOP, but most of them also tried to make an explicit connection between LWOP and dying in prison in order to equate LWOP to a death sentence. For example, in their opening statement, Donald's defense team told the jury, "[Donald] will leave jail in a coffin. He will come out feet first, one way or the other …" In Roger's trial, the defense stated in their opening, "The only way he'll leave prison will be in a coffin," and in Ted's case, the defense attorney stated, "And the verdict, in essence, has already sentenced—resulted in a sentence of death for [Ted]. He will die in prison." A similar connection was made in Alan's case when the defense attorney stated, "This man (indicating) has, in essence, already been condemned. He's going to spend the rest of his life in jail or you're going to give him the death penalty. He dies in prison or he dies in prison mandated by your order." In Steve's trial, the argument was made that by convicting the defendant of first degree murder, the jury had already "guaranteed that [Steve] will spend the rest of his life in jail. Our law does not allow for probation and parole in these cases and as a result [Steve] is looking at dying in jail." In line with the arguments of other defenders who tried to equate a LWOP sentence with a death sentence, Steve's lawyer went on to state in the closing argument that by convicting Steve they had "already imposed a death sentence on [Steve]. Because of that verdict, [Steve] is going to die in jail." This connection between LWOP and death was seen again in Charlie's trial, where the argument was made that "… he is going to die in jail. He will never be released from imprisonment. … In some ways, it can be said that a sentence of life imprisonment in actuality and the death penalty are similar in some respects because under both scenarios, the person dies in jail." Attorneys in *all eight trials* used both their opening and closing statements at the penalty phase to tell jurors that the defendant was condemned to spend the rest of his life behind bars whether he eventually gets a lethal injection or succumbs to some other cause of death.

He Won't Be a Danger

Once establishing that LWOP means what it says, the attorneys set out to demonstrate that LWOP would be sufficient to protect the public or to punish the offender sufficiently for his deeds. In two of the eight trials (one that ended with a death verdict and one that ended with a life verdict), an expert was called *explicitly* to offer his or her opinion that the defendant would not be a threat in prison, but even when no expert witnesses were called to describe the incapacitating abilities of prison, the attorneys made a declaration during opening or closing statements that their clients would not be a danger behind bars.

Jerry's mitigation case included a psychologist who was specifically asked to testify about Jerry's mental condition in order to suggest that Jerry could "make a relatively successful adjustment to prison …" and that he would not pose a threat to correctional officers, visitors, other inmates, or other individuals in the prison. During his testimony, the psychologist cited studies that concluded that most violent offenders do *not* commit acts of violence while in prison. He explained that prison has restrictions that prevent violence and that the murder rate in prison is lower than it is in free society. He then concluded his testimony by opining that "it's not very likely that, given the restrictions in prison, that he would be a danger to society in prison," and in the summation, Jerry's attorneys summarized this testimony to suggest that Jerry would not be "a threat of future violence." This testimony and the accompanying closing argument seem to take as a given that Jerry would be a threat to society unless society incapacitates him in some way. It does not focus on the importance of social context, environmental factors, or the defendant's life history. Rather, the major focus of this testimony was on the ability of prison to prevent offenders from committing acts of violence even if they want to.

In Alan's mitigation case, the second one in which an expert was called explicitly to discuss the defendant's future dangerousness while in prison, there was a shift toward the importance of social context for making decisions, but the major focus remained on the ability of prison to incapacitate the offender. The forensic psychologist opined, "He's the kind of person that in a highly structured situation he could function well and follow what he has to do ..." A little later, he said, "So overall, his personality, there was nothing pointing that there was any kind of a serious problem or I would consider him as a dangerous person, danger to himself or danger to others in the environment that he's in now." Towards the end of his testimony, the psychologist again suggested that because of the defendant's "personality profile ... he can function in a highly structured environment." Although there is some mention of environmental factors in this testimony, the predominant focus was on Alan's "personality" and whether or not he was the kind of person who could conform to the rigors of prison life. It was not about how social context can influence decision-making processes; instead the testimony was about how well Alan's personality traits would enable him to adjust to prison. In fact, there was no discussion regarding how Alan's previous behavior may have been impacted by his social environment, nor was there a suggestion that his new environment would change him. Instead, the implication was that, given his personality, prison would be able to control him.

In general, however, experts were not called explicitly to tell jurors that prison would keep defendants from being violent in the future. It was usually left to the attorneys to remind jurors in their opening and closing statements that the defendants really would spend life in prison and to assuage the fear of jurors that they might get out one day. For example, in the opening statement, Michael's defense attorney told the jury that Michael "would not be a danger to others if imprisoned at maximum security for the rest of his life as a result of the verdict that you've already handed down." In the closing argument presented by Roger's defense attorney, it was suggested that, "Our community is protected from [Roger] by keeping him in jail until he dies. And when you realize that, then I ask you to consider that his execution would serve no other purpose than retribution."

Overall the transcripts reveal that the ability of LWOP to incapacitate the defendant—who may or may not remain a dangerous person—was a key ingredient in these eight mitigation cases. Interestingly, this discussion often played right into the prosecution's strategy of focusing the case solely on the defendant's murderous behavior or his evil personality. While the strategy of arguing that LWOP can also incapacitate may have been a good one if it assuaged jurors' fears that the defendant might be released, it also probably reinforced the dominant narrative of individual culpability by focusing on the defendant's individual dangerousness and describing the defendant as a dangerous person in need of restraint rather than as a social creature whose behavior is greatly impacted by social circumstances.

Life is Just as Retributive

In five of the cases, the attorneys supplemented the "LWOP can incapacitate" rationale with an argument that LWOP was as retributive as a death sentence and was therefore sufficiently severe to punish the offender for his crime. The line of thinking here remains in line with hegemonic individualism in that it still treats the defendants as "monadic, self-authored" (Dunn and Kaplan, 2009, p. 341) and autonomous individuals who deserve to be punished instead of as social creatures acting "within particular socio-historical contexts that limit perceived and material possibilities for action" (Dunn and Kaplan, 2009, p. 364). As Roger's defense attorney argued, "It's going to be an empty life. He'll have nothing to look forward to. His girlfriend will abandon him. He'll just sit there with the world going by, just waiting, waiting to die." Michael's lawyer told the judge and jury that no sentence would bring the victim back but that the defendant's life in prison would probably include "the harshest conditions that prison has to offer." He said Michael would no longer be able to go dancing, drink alcohol, or have girlfriends. Stressing that nothing could ease the pain of the victim's family, Donald's attorney told jurors, "[Donald] will be severely punished. There is no doubt about that." In a fourth case, Ted's lawyer told the judge and jury, "If he is sentenced to life in prison without the possibility of parole or probation, he will have every day of the rest of his life to think; think about what he's done; think about what he hasn't done in his life; think about what he cannot do with his life …" Finally, Steve's defense attorney did some math for the jurors and explained, "If he lives to be 75 years old and then he dies in jail, he will have served a 56-year prison sentence. Isn't that punishment enough for this crime?"

In all five cases, the quoted passages were the only times the attorneys presented the argument that LWOP was as retributive as (or perhaps more retributive than) the death penalty, and in each case, the major thrust of the argument was focused on incapacitation: life really means life so the defendant will never be released from prison to victimize innocent civilians again. In none of these passages was there a discussion of whether the defendant deserved harsh punishment or if he was not entirely to blame for the outcome. There was not a suggestion that the defendant may not deserve death because there were factors beyond his control that may have impacted his actions. Rather, the argument is that the defendant can be spared because LWOP is just as harsh as—or perhaps harsher than—the death penalty. By suggesting that LWOP is sufficient to avenge the victim's death, the defense attorneys indirectly supported vengeance as a legitimate punishment philosophy and directed attention to individual responsibility attribution and away from social causation, a move that validates both "the ideology of individualism that fuels their client's social exclusion" (Dunn and Kaplan, 2009, p. 360) and the existence of the death penalty. After all, if LWOP is just as retributive as a death sentence and LWOP is a legitimate punishment option, then so too is death.

Conclusion

The trial transcripts reveal that in many ways, Dunn and Kaplan are right that "individualism is so embedded in our social interventions and the law that it is practically impossible to talk about particular subjects in capital cases without reinforcing and valorizing it" (2009, p. 339). All eight mitigation cases in this sample relied on individualizing arguments, most notably the argument that the defendant simply lacked the requisite state of mind to be executed—he was either just an accomplice or did not really intend the victim's death. Furthermore, they argued that LWOP was a sufficient enough penalty to either incapacitate the defendant or avenge the victim. In the process, they may have been inadvertently supporting the anti-sociological commonsense understanding of human behavior that justifies the death penalty in the first place because both of these lines of reasoning focus on the offender as an individual divorced from his social context and ask what he deserves for his crime—not what social forces also contributed to this crime that might be relevant for understanding how or why it occurred. The basic argument being presented was that the defendant's murderous actions (regardless of whatever environmental or contextual forces may have influenced his decisions or behavior) were not bad enough to warrant a death sentence or that a LWOP sentence is sufficiently severe to accomplish the same sentencing goals as a death sentence. The focus of these arguments was to determine whether the defendant had "full or diminished agency based on personal characteristics" (Dunn and Kaplan, 2009, p. 364) that are located completely *within* the defendant; outside influences were of no relevance to this inquiry. In this sense, these arguments clearly and unmistakably reinforce and instantiate individualism.

These findings are not a criticism of the defense attorneys or mitigation experts in these trials. Rather, they illuminate the power of hegemonic tales. Capital defense attorneys have an ethical and moral obligation to do everything in their power to spare their clients. As Galanter (1974) has explained, unlike repeat players who can play for rules and can sacrifice a few cases for favorable rulings down the road, attorneys who represent "one-shotters"—those with only occasional interactions with the court—cannot play the long game. They cannot sacrifice one case for more favorable outcomes down the road. They must act in the best interests of each individual client. Since the existing literature and the findings revealed in Chapters 4 and 5 indicate that jurors and judges appear more likely to respond to individualizing mitigators, attorneys who challenge the basic tenets of psychological individualism may be placing their clients at greater risk (even if such challenges reduce the use of the death penalty at some hypothetical future point). Therefore, in order to construct a mitigation case that is likely to meet with the approval of those who will decide if their clients live or die, defense attorneys are compelled to utilize individualizing arguments that support a worldview that fuels the very existence of capital punishment.

Chapter 3
Subversive Stories in Capital Mitigation

> "… a person's free will should only be judged in the context of the person's life. We are, to a large extent, the products of our environment."

> "… people just aren't plain evil; that otherwise good kids can end up being at risk to do violence from many factors outside their control …"

While the findings in Chapter 2 show the power of hegemonic narratives to compel defense attorneys to rely upon individualizing stories, this view of mitigation is incomplete. Mitigation is far too complex and nuanced to support a simple conclusion that mitigation supports hegemonic individualism. As noted in Chapter 2, capital defense attorneys utilized a multi-pronged approach in their mitigation cases that often interwove subversive stories with individualistic ones. In fact, it appears that most defense lawyers were trying to offer stories that could challenge the taken-for-granted beliefs about individual responsibility and help to educate jurors about the impact past experiences and current social contexts can have on one's decisions and behaviors. In five of the eight trials, the mitigation cases challenged the psy-complex's individualistic explanations by using the testimony of mitigation experts to present contextualized biographical narratives that attempted to demonstrate the powerful influence of external forces on the defendants' formation, and in all eight cases, family members and friends of the defendant were called to testify in order to humanize the defendant and to imbed him within a web of social relationships by showing how much they loved him and would be hurt by his execution and to attest to all of the positive things he had done in his life. This was an attempt to subvert the idea that the defendants' characters can be understood by knowing that they murdered and to show that they are capable of both good deeds and bad deeds depending on the circumstance. Combined, these two mitigating themes served to challenge the taken-for-granted assumptions of individualism that killers are just evil-doers bent on destruction.

"Not Born a Natural-Born Killer": Subverting Hegemonic Discourses

In five of these eight trials, an expert social worker or forensic nurse was called to the stand for the express purpose of testifying as to the impact factors beyond the defendant's control had on his subsequent behavior. In each instance, they challenged the assumptions of retributive individualism by trying to connect the defendant's past experiences to his subsequent behavior and showing how and why he was at an elevated risk for committing violent acts due to factors over which he had no control. These experts explained how the presence or absence of certain factors in one's life make one more or less likely to commit violence and attempted to demonstrate how events impact everyone differently depending on a complex confluence of circumstances that come to characterize one's life history. In other words, the trial transcripts clearly show that defense attorneys are not entirely beholden to individualism. Although they are compelled to make individualizing arguments, they are also able and willing to present contextualizing mitigation that subverts the cultural master narrative. In fact, they were imploring jurors to look outside the box of individualism, to set aside their commonsense understandings of human behavior as a matter of a purely free will, and to try to comprehend how social conditions influenced the horrible decisions of their clients.

Contextualizing Mitigation in Life Cases

Donald: "Factors Outside Their Control"

As explained in Chapter 2, Donald was convicted of felony murder but acquitted of intentional murder because it was not clear whether he or a co-perpetrator fired the fatal shot, and his defense lawyers used this doubt in their mitigation case to suggest Donald was not culpable enough to deserve death. However, within their mitigation case, they also attempted to subvert the individualistic story by offering the testimony of two social workers who testified as to Donald's upbringing and how this created an increase risk of violent behavior. As stated in the opening statement:

> [Risk factors will be used] to try to give you an understanding of why this person is the way they are today.
>
> And these risk factors are factors that are *outside the control of the person* who is at risk. They're things that he *didn't have any control over*. And as I said, they're not excuses. They're offered to help you understand why this person might be in a situation he's in as opposed to another person (emphasis added).

During the penalty hearing, one social worker testified as to Donald's social history, and in an attempt to use this history to contextualize Donald's subsequent behavior, the second social worker utilized a study published by the Department of Justice (DOJ) entitled *Child Delinquents: Development, Intervention, and Service Needs* that identified a long list of risk factors for future violence and protective factors that could help counter-balance the risk factors. The risk factors were grouped into four categories: individual, family, peer-related, and school and community-related (Loeber and Farrington, 2001; Wasserman et al., 2003). The use of this report is indicative of the defense's intent to subvert hegemonic discourses because the report specifically states that "there is abundant evidence that factors in the child's social environment influence long-term outcomes" and even addresses the argument made by many supporters of individualism that many people who experience certain risk factors do not end up being violent: "No single risk factor explains juvenile delinquency. Rather, the higher the number of risk factors ... the higher the likelihood of early onset-offending. ... Although there are some risk factors that are common to child delinquents, the pattern and particular combination of risk factors may vary from child to child" (Loeber and Farrington, 2001, p. xxvi).

The report even included a statistical analysis of how much more likely those who experienced each factor were to become violent than those who did not have the same experience. The statistical analysis is important because it helps to demonstrate the complexity of social causation and show that sociological evidence is not equivalent to environmental determinism. Many critics of social theories of crime (including academic critics) base their arguments on the incontrovertible fact that not everyone with a certain background turns out to be a criminal (Samenow, 2004; Wilson, 1975). However, such arguments misrepresent what social theories say. Unlike theories in the natural sciences that would predict the same outcome every time, social theories recognize the complexity of the social world, understand that every single person is unique (unlike water molecules, for example, which are all identical), and do not suggest that every person will be affected in the same way by the same factor. Because no two persons have the exact same set of experiences (including identical twins), very few (if any) social influences will have the same impact on all who experience them (Haney, 1995). Therefore, social theories are not about showing direct causation or even necessary or sufficient causation; they are concerned with recognizing and explaining social patterns and probabilities. For example, not everyone who smokes will develop lung cancer and some people who never smoke will develop lung cancer, but this does not mean that smoking is unrelated to the chances of getting lung cancer. In the same way, not everyone who grows up poor and abused will go on to commit murder. Contextualizing mitigation, therefore, is not about showing inevitability; rather, it is about assessing the formative importance of prior experiences. Thus, the report's use of statistical probabilities is a key ingredient in constructing a subversive narrative that offers a useable alternative to the hegemonic tale of autonomous individualism.

During her testimony, the social worker explained to the judge and jury that Donald experienced numerous risk factors for future violence identified in the DOJ report, most of which were beyond his control, and that his life was relatively devoid of protective factors. These risk factors included parental criminality, poor family management factors, low levels of parental involvement, poor family bonding, family conflict, parental attitudes favorable to substance abuse and violence, residential mobility, parent/child separation, academic failure, low bonding to school, truancy, involvement with antisocial peers, availability of drugs and firearms, neighborhood adults involved in crime, and violence in the neighborhood. Conversely, only a single protective factor was identified: pro-social grandparents. In the penalty trial, Donald's defense team presented evidence that Donald was born to young unwed parents and that soon after his birth, his mother became addicted to crack. Since his father was not involved in his life, this forced him to live with his grandmother despite the fact that she was ill-equipped to raise him in the high-crime and violent neighborhood in which she lived. The social workers even testified in detail how these factors led the defendant to associate with anti-social peers beginning at a young age. In second grade, the defendant lived with his mother for a bit while she was recovering but this was in a drug-infested area, which exposed Donald to a drug lifestyle at a young age and caused his mother to relapse. While living there, the defendant was also exposed to physical violence exhibited by his mother's boyfriends. After his mother's arrest for drug use, the defendant moved back in with his grandmother, but Donald still began associating with the wrong crowd because his grandmother was not capable of properly supervising him in the neighborhood in which she resided. Following his association with an older group of men, Donald started using drugs himself and became involved in more serious crimes. He was even incarcerated as a juvenile for a violent offense. The first social worker testified that the defendant "thrived" on the structure he was afforded while in prison but that he "flounders" when deprived of that structure at his grandmother's house, suggesting that context is important. When he is in a disciplined and structured environment, he is able to conform, but when left without guidance or discipline, he encounters problems.

The social workers presented the case that Donald was not inherently bad and that given the right opportunities, he could conform and be a good person. Unfortunately, negative influences and other factors beyond his control led him down a path of crime and drug dealing. As explained by one of the social workers, the risk factors Donald experienced were "For the most part, not in [Donald's] control," and in an attempt to combat the argument that these risk factors are meaningless because some people experience them and do not become violent, she also testified as to the defendant's relative lack of protective factors and pointed out how the existence of such factors can blunt the impact of risk factors. To hammer home the point that there are external forces at work influencing everyone's behavior, the defense attorney summarized this testimony in his closing arguments and suggested that the evidence indicates "that people just aren't plain evil; that otherwise good kids can end up being at risk to do violence from many factors *outside their control* ..." (emphasis added). He then asked the jurors to consider how Donald would have turned out if he had not been exposed to so many negative experiences.

Roger: "Products of our Environment"

Similarly, the mitigation case in Roger's trial also attempted to contextualize Roger's life experiences. Again, the attorneys in Roger's trial did try to cast doubt on his culpability. As mentioned in Chapter 2, Roger was convicted of killing an acquaintance during a robbery, but the defense tried to suggest two other men were involved and potentially more blameworthy than Roger. However, Roger's defense team also told a subversive tale of a childhood that greatly impacted Roger and made it "almost inevitable that this was going to happen."

In the opening statement, Roger's attorney described Roger's life history, which included numerous factors beyond his control, such as residential mobility and being surrounded by crime, drugs, and violence as a young child. Utilizing the same DOJ study that was used in Donald's trial, two social workers testified as to the large number of risk factors to which Roger was exposed and explained how these factors likely affected his behavior. These risk factors included parental criminality, child maltreatment, witnessing domestic violence, poor family management factors, low levels of parental involvement, poor family bonding and family conflict, parental attitudes favorable to substance use and violence, residential mobility, parent/child separation, academic failure, low bonding to school, truancy and dropping out, frequent school transitions, delinquent family and peers, poverty, community disorganization, availability of drugs and firearms, and neighborhood adults involved in crime. According to the testimony, Roger moved more than once a year during his early childhood; witnessed domestic abuse; attended a failing school system; had an absent father; had many family members involved in drugs and crime; and grew up in one of the poorest, most disorganized, crime-infested, and drug-riddled cities in the nation. Very few of these factors were within the control of Roger. Especially as a child, he had little power to alter any of these conditions.

The expert testimony then attempted to challenge the commonsense wisdom that people can pull themselves up by the bootstraps by explaining, "I strongly believe that what happens to you when children is—is critical in understanding how you turn out as an adult." In addressing the question begged by the use of the DOJ study and the focus on risk factors for criminality—namely, why are there people who are at significant risk of criminality that do not offend—the social worker stated, "[P]rotective factors can help balance out risk factors," but Roger had very few protective factors.

It is significant that very few of these risk factors had anything to do with Roger's psychology, internal functioning, or personal choices because it afforded the defense team an opportunity to explicitly challenge the basic tenets of psychological individualism. First, they asked the jury to consider how one can be affected by prior experiences:

> How did [Roger] develop his character and propensities? Is he a bad seed, more than evil, with no hope of redemption? I think anyone who looks at those baby pictures will know that's not the case. So, the question is then, how was his character shaped by the facts and circumstances of his life?

They then suggest to the jury that none of the risk factors that shaped Roger's character were within his control:

> Was it [Roger]'s fault that his mother was a 16-year-old teenager without an education or money or stable home? Was it his fault that his biological father rejected him his entire life, that his biological father wouldn't even cooperate

> with his defense team in preparing this case? Or is it [Roger]'s fault that he was a witness and the victim of domestic abuse? Is it his fault that the vast majority of his relatives were drug abusers, criminals, or both; that by the time he was 13, he lived in 15 different places; and that, in the first eight years of his schooling, he attended six different schools? Is it his fault he grew up in [city], a high crime city, where the school quality was so low, that the State had to come in and take over? Can you understand how, under those circumstances, he [had] trouble making the right friends, develop[ing] meaningful positive relationships?
>
> I submit that the evidence has shown that [Roger]'s early-life exposure to these risk factors provides the explanation for why he grew up without the moral compass to point him in the right direction. The serious negative impact of these risk factors during his formative years affected his ability to make the right decisions as an adult.

They conclude this part of their summation by telling jurors they need to abandon their commonsense views of individual responsibility: "I hope that our community recognizes that children who suffer a childhood exposed to domestic violence, drug abuse, and criminal activity have a hard time choosing the right path in life. The studies commissioned by the federal Department of Justice support that fact."

Far from supporting hegemonic individualism, the argument that was presented here tried to get jurors to rethink their commonsense beliefs about free will and individual responsibility by viewing the entire biography of Roger's life and the ways in which his choices were impacted by events in his past. It is true that at other points in the penalty phase, the defense tried to suggest that Roger did not deserve death because of his culpability relative to what the defense tried to suggest were accomplices. However, in this instance, the primary argument made by the defense team was that taken-for-granted beliefs about individual responsibility are not valid. As stated later in the defense's summation:

> … A person's free will should only be judged in the context of the person's life. We are, to a large extent, the products of our environment. … To think that, because other people have overcome obstacles, we should kill [Roger] because he didn't, is fundamentally unfair. Not everyone reacts the same to obstacles.

It is hard to envision an argument that more directly or accurately challenges hegemonic individualism.

Ted: "Other People Couldn't Have Made Different Choices"

Ted's case reveals a similar mitigation strategy. As was explained in Chapter 2, his attorneys did attempt to mitigate his punishment by focusing on his lack of intent and telling the jury that he was only convicted of negligently killing the victim during a botched robbery because the victim resisted and grabbed the gun. Yet, they did not stop there. They offered other stories that both challenged and supported hegemonic individualism. For example, a psychologist testified on Ted's behalf and described the internal problems Ted experienced in a manner quite consistent with what Dunn and Kaplan (2009) would have predicted. However, the psychologist also explained how childhood experiences affect one's adult decisions, and the defense also called a forensic nurse to describe the myriad of negative experiences Ted had in his childhood. So while they acknowledged that Ted made choices, they also argued that given his set of experiences, "[P]erhaps other people couldn't have made different decisions."

The defense psychologist told the jury that Ted suffered from some internal problems, such as bipolar disorder, attention deficit hyperactivity disorder (ADHD), poor spelling and arithmetic skills, poor judgment, and thinking problems. However, he tried to suggest that some of these problems were related to past experiences. For example, he told the jury that Ted's paranoia was at least partially the result of witnessing his father repeatedly abusing his mother and living in an impoverished area characterized by high levels of street crime. He described Ted's early childhood experiences as "chaotic" and then explained that human beings are a combination "of our experiences and our heredity." The following day, a forensic nurse testified as to this "chaotic" childhood, which included physical abuse, neglect, his father abusing his mother (physically and sexually), psychological abuse, personal rejection, discovering his father was dating while married to his mother, repeating third and sixth grade, having his home burglarized by his father, two house fires (the second of which was deliberately set by his father), the death of his older sister, the introduction of her young children into the household, and learning of his father's illegitimate child and the resulting family friction.

During her testimony, the nurse described how the defendant was an unwanted child who was frequently abused and neglected, and during the testimony of Ted's mother, she admitted that neither she nor her husband wanted another child when she got pregnant with Ted and that Ted's father would often say that Ted was not his son and refuse to take part in his life. Ted's mother was also abused by her husband constantly, including while she was pregnant with Ted. Ted's father raped her regularly, verbally abused her in front of the children, threatened to kill her, and even pointed a gun at her head twice. The defense psychologist testified that Ted experienced a chaotic and traumatic childhood, which caused him to develop paranoia and an extreme fear of abandonment. During critical formative years, Ted was badly neglected, which prevented him from developing trust or self-control. As a child, the defendant was always afraid and wanted to sleep in bed with his mother, but when his father was home, he would chase Ted out of the room, and Ted would end up sleeping outside the bedroom door. After chasing his son out, Ted's father would often argue with his wife about babying Ted and then rape her as punishment. These and other events caused Ted to be so afraid of his father that when he was eight years old, a burn on his upper leg went untreated for two days because he was afraid to admit that he spilled scalding soup on himself when he was supposed to be in bed.

The forensic nurse also explained that Ted's mother refused to allow him to get treatment for his ADHD because she feared the side effects of the medication; this resulted in acting out and school failure. Ted's father would even swing by Ted's school frequently, and when he saw Ted misbehaving, he would take him out of school, beat him with a belt, and return him to school despite the pleas of Ted's teachers, who tried to explain that his behavior was the result of his ADHD. In addition to this mistreatment, Ted's father also dated other women while still married to Ted's mother. Even after his father moved out, the terrorism and abuse did not stop. After leaving the house, Ted's father burglarized it, stealing everything of value, and another time, he set the house on fire. As the youngest child (and the unwanted one), Ted experienced these events more poignantly and acutely than the other children, and at around the same time that all of this was happening, Ted was diagnosed with asthma, placed in special education, and began failing in school. He had to repeat the third and sixth grades.

The defense's social worker even relayed a story about how Ted was abandoned on his father's doorstep in the rain at the age of 11. At this point, Ted's mother had left his father and since his father had destroyed their house, they were living with Ted's maternal grandmother in a one-bedroom apartment. Ted's older sister then died, and her children came to live with the family, along with his father's illegitimate 18-year-old daughter. These new responsibilities distracted Ted's mother's attention away from Ted. She also no longer had room for him in the one-bedroom apartment she now shared with these children and her own mother. The apartment was in a bad area, so Ted's mother decided Ted should live with his father. Rather than discussing the situation with his father, his mother took him over to his father's house, knocked on the door and told the father he had to take care of his son:

> So his mother decided that it would be best for him to live with [his father]. And she tried to negotiate that with [his father] and took [Ted] over with his clothes, and knocked on [father]'s door and said, "Here is your son. You've got to take him. I don't want him in that neighborhood."
>
> And [father] said, "He's your son. You wanted him. You can take care of him," and shut the door.
>
> And [mother] said she thought that he was just being mean to her. So she left [Ted] on the porch and she left.
>
> Apparently, [father] got in his car and left, left [Ted] outside, and it was raining. He left him outside. And [Ted] went to a neighbor and the neighbor, I guess tried to call [father]. And, finally, someone—I don't know—[mother] thinks it was probably [father] that did it—called Child Protective, and Child Protective took [Ted] and investigated it …

This event left a huge emotional scar on Ted and made him feel like neither parent wanted him. Compounding his problems, Child Protective Services placed Ted back with his mother, who was still living in the same cramped one-bedroom apartment with her mother and caring for other people's children. There was simply no room for Ted. With no place to sleep, Ted would often claim he was going to a friend's house, but in reality he was spending nights on the street and sneaking back home during the day (when no one was home) to sleep instead of attending school.

The nurse's framing of Ted's problems were as external ones beyond his control, and she described Ted as being "really impacted" by the experience of being left on his father's porch. It was shown that Ted did not make the choice to roam the streets at night, where he began to associate with bad influences. Rather, "it just became too crowded in the house. There were fights over the bathroom and fights over space." Ted was forced to choose among sleeping on the floor with mice (which scared him), sleeping on the couch with his mother, sleeping with his grandmother, or staying out all night. His options were constrained. Unfortunately, these forced choices caused him to begin associating with neighborhood children who introduced him to a world of crime and drugs.

Yet, when placed in a more structured environment due to truancy, Ted was able to thrive according to the nurse. He did extremely well and his grades improved, but as he neared discharge, he started acting up again in an attempt to avoid being sent back home. Although he appeared to be happy and thriving in the structured environment provided by his alternative school, after being sent back home, "he trailed back off again." Being back in his old environment, Ted began using marijuana again, stopped going to school, and started associating with drug dealers. By age 17, Ted was discharged from school because he had too many failures and was not attending. He started abusing alcohol around this time, and at the age of 18, he left his mother's house and began living with friends or on the street, descending into a life of crime. All of this testimony was designed to demonstrate the importance of social environment, and the defense attorneys said just this in their closing remarks to the judge and jury. They described Ted's childhood as "nightmares," but rather than originating inside of Ted, they all were caused by external forces.

Contextualizing Mitigation in Death Cases

Interestingly, in the two death cases that used expert testimony to present contextual evidence, there was little difference in strategy or presentation compared to the life cases. The defense attempted to diminish the defendant's culpability but also supplemented this effort with a subversive story of how the defendant's experiences as a child significantly impacted his later choices in life.

Steve: "A Chaotic Environment"

Steve's trial is indicative of this process. In Chapter 2, it was explained that Steve was involved in the murder of two teens but that he was working under the direction and influence of an older co-perpetrator and that no evidence could establish who fired the fatal bullets. This doubt was a key element of the mitigation case, but so too was Steve's chaotic childhood. In their opening statement, Steve's defense team explained that they were going to use a psychologist and a social worker to show the judge and jury why Steve was "at high risk to commit violent acts" and how this evidence would be important to help them "understand how a child at risk, a childlike [*sic*] [Steve] is molded into [someone] who makes horribly wrong choices."

First through the testimony of a social worker, the defense tried to paint a picture for the judge and jury that "what happens to people when they are children matters tremendously as to how they turn out as adults." After describing Steve's past, the social worker reviewed the DOJ study on risk and protective factors mentioned above and explained all the risk factors Steve had, placing his life into context. The risk factors described by the social worker include having a number of relatives—including parents—with long criminal records or histories of drug abuse; low levels of parental involvement, including the fact that his parents were teenagers when he was born and his father has not been in his life since he was three years old; that "his mother had several relationships and brought various father figures into his life;" witnessing his mother being abused while he was a child; his family's failure to properly supervise him and set appropriate standards; poor family bonding and family conflict; parental attitudes favorable to substance abuse and violence; instability in that his primary caretaker shifted among his mother, his grandmother; the co-perpetrator, and other relatives; low bonding to school and frequent school transitions; delinquent peers; availability of drugs and firearms in the neighborhood and in the home; exposure to violence in the community and neighborhood; low levels of emotional support and mental stimulation as a child; and poverty.

These factors existed in the world into which Steve was born; they were not part of his individualized pathology. For example, Steve received little love, support, or validation in his life until he met the co-perpetrator, who appears to have profoundly influenced his behavior as an almost surrogate father figure. As in Roger's case, the social worker explained that these factors were not determinative but that those who experience such factors are more likely to become violent and that the more risk factors one has relative to the number of protective factors, the greater the risk. She presented statistics that indicated that not everyone with a given experience became a criminal, just that they were more likely to do so. The social worker then opined that "family history and family assessment is a factor that explains why he is the way he is as an adult."

The defense's psychologist supported the social worker's contextual story by explaining "how all experiences can have an impact on us as we go through life." The psychologist testified that he was trying "to understand what sort of impact [Steve's experiences] had on [him]"and suggested that if it was not for the influence of the co-perpetrator, Steve would likely not have acted in the way he did. He only did so because this was the only person who ever gave him any sense of validation. As mentioned above, Steve's real father was a teenager when Steve was born and was never involved in Steve's life. Throughout his life, Steve's mother had several relationships with other men, but it was not until she began dating the co-perpetrator that Steve became connected to any of them as a father figure. The defense psychologist explained to the jury that Steve "needs a lot of evidence that this good picture he has painted of himself is really the true one and not this other one. So he becomes dependant [*sic*] upon the validation and affirmation of other people who are important to him." Unfortunately, Steve "had a close relationship with an individual who was an important source of support in the form of [co-perpetrator] and I believe that he provided him with a lot[of] the sense of validation as well. And part of the dilemma was when [co-perpetrator] started to give him validation that was in part based on him doing very, very awful things" (including a prior murder). The psychologist went on to suggest that when Steve "gets into situations where his emotions become aroused … it is hard for him to sort through what should I do? How should I handle it? What decision should I make?" In these types of situations, the influence "of the person that can give him validation" becomes extremely powerful and can cause Steve to behave in manners that he otherwise would not have acted because "[i]t is hard to run from the person [from] whom you get your emotional sustenance." Furthermore, the psychologist told the judge and jury that this feature of Steve is not something he was born with; rather, it is the result of having "grown up in a chaotic environment."

Charlie: "An Unwanted Child"

Charlie's mitigation case reflected more of the individualizing themes identified in Dunn and Kaplan's (2009) study, but they also went beyond this presentation to point out that he became the person he is through experiences over which he had no control. Charlie killed a young child with a stray bullet while gunning down a rival. As described in Chapter 2, part of the mitigation case involved arguing that Charlie did not intend to kill the child. Furthermore, Charlie's defense team also presented life history evidence that relied on individualizing discourse. This evidence pointed to Charlie's limited mental abilities, substance abuse problems, learning disorders, clinical depression, head injuries, school failure, and self-esteem and mood problems. From an early age, Charlie had significant problems, including cognitive limitations and a delay in developing both motor skills and an ability to interpret and respond to his circumstances. School was frustrating for him, and there was evidence presented that Charlie was clinically depressed at an early age, that he had learning disorders, and a history of head injuries. Reports indicated that Charlie had limited mental ability; an IQ in the low 80s; substance abuse problems; and difficulty predicting consequences, assessing social situations, or solving practical problems. However, the mitigation case did not stop there. Instead, it was suggested that Charlie needed interventions throughout his life that he was denied and that if he had received them or if he had a more supportive home environment, he would have been a significantly different person.

Instead of placing the onus of Charlie's behavior completely within the borders of Charlie, Charlie's defense attorney tried to suggest that much of what caused Charlie's problems were things outside of Charlie:

> Is [Charlie] an evil person that was begotten evil and is evil to this day, or is [Charlie] somebody who may be a sad individual, who may have had some problems, who may have had some benefits, at least materialistic trappings and appearances that everything was okay, but to a large extent was neglected and never got what was required for him?

Unlike "Daniel," who was "continually described as inherently and individually 'bad'" (Dunn and Kaplan, 2009, p. 354), Charlie was described as someone who ended up the way he did because of life experiences over which he had no control. Through Charlie's mother and stepfather, a social worker, and a psychiatrist, the defense presented a troubling life history that included developmental problems, counseling, and a severe descent upon learning that his stepfather was not his biological father. Even though many of Charlie's problems were described as cognitive limitations, such as being diagnosed with multiple mental disorders that required special education throughout his school career and professional counseling beginning at an early age, Charlie's records suggested that he needed "fairly intensive efforts pretty young" and that numerous experts expressed this opinion along the way. However, despite clear warning signs as a child, Charlie's parents did not always act in his best interests. They did not take the advice of his counselors, they placed him in Kindergarten early, they did not get him needed counseling, and they insisted he be removed from special education despite his limited mental ability, which led to school failure and self-esteem and other mood problems. The social worker concluded that she was "inclined to think it would have made a difference if he had had a sounder environment that supported his needs and found constructive ways for him to identify himself." Rather than the result of individual characteristics, Charlie's behavior was shown to be related to the environment in which he was raised. His failure to get those interventions was not a result of his own choosing but his parents' poor decisions. The defense's psychiatrist supported this position. Although most of his testimony described problems of individual psychological problems, he also indicated that Charlie's problems went beyond just his internal cognitive impairments. He explained that the defendant lacked emotional support and felt betrayed. These external factors played an important role in shaping Charlie's antisocial behavior. Like the social worker, the psychiatrist lamented that Charlie did not receive needed treatment as a young child.

The social worker also explained that Charlie lacked positive male role models, that he "functioned as sort of an unwanted child," and that he lacked emotional supports. These problems were exacerbated when, against the advice of counselors, Charlie's mother informed him that her husband was not his biological father. The social worker described this revelation as the major event in Charlie's life. This discovery triggered distrust and a sense of rejection: "We're talking about a child who ... experienced what, to the present day, he regards as one of the most primary experiences in his life, which was learning that the person he had perceived as his birth father was not, and that this was a traumatic breach of trust for him." The social worker went on to say that Charlie insisted that he be taken to meet his father. Unfortunately, Charlie met his father "at a fairly impressionable age," and the father, who had recently gotten out of prison, only had negative things to say to him and "glamorized ... the perception of a criminal lifestyle ..." The breach of trust associated with this discovery and other events around the same time convinced the defendant that everyone hated him, and he began associating with the wrong crowd and getting into legal trouble. Overall, the expert testimony contextualized Charlie's character, suggesting that structured environments would allow him to function better, that a sounder home environment could have made a difference in his life, that not receiving needed counseling made things worse, and that he only turned to the street because he was unable to find acceptance elsewhere, which caused him to begin valuing himself based upon his street skills. Summing up all of this testimony, Charlie's attorney argued in his closing argument,

> [Charlie] was not born a natural-born killer. [Charlie] became the person he is through his life experiences. He was a person who had a lot of limitations. He was a person who had a lot of difficulties. He was a person who experienced some things as a child *over which he had no control, no control whatsoever* (emphasis added).

A Note on Contextual Mitigation in Michael's Trial

There was also an attempt to contextualize Michael's behavior, but Michael's attorneys did not use any expert witnesses to try to contextualize his behavior. The only evidence of his past came from second-hand accounts told by family members who had no knowledge of his whereabouts during his most critical formative experiences. Therefore, it was difficult for Michael's attorneys to connect his prior experiences to the crime of which he was just convicted. Michael's father explained that he and Michael's mother were both teenagers when Michael was born and that Michael lived with his mother, who abused drugs, was a little wild, and would often leave Michael unattended in a car while she would go out partying. The father would get to visit Michael every other weekend, but one weekend when Michael was 11-years-old, he went to pick up Michael and discovered the house vacant. He had no contact with his son or knowledge of his whereabouts for 13 years, when Michael contacted him from prison. While living with his mother in another state, Michael's mother had a string of boyfriends who verbally and physically abused him, including one who would lock him in a closet. One of Michael's aunts testified that Michael ran away from his mother at the age of 15 due to unbearable conditions and ended up running around with a bad crowd. The defendant did not contact his paternal family when he first got into legal trouble because he feared that his mother would find him and make him return. However, there were no witnesses from Michael's time out of state to corroborate these stories, so it is difficult to draw any definitive conclusions regarding his past.

Most significantly, Michael did not utilize a single expert to explain why any of this evidence was relevant. In the defense's opening statement, they gave a brief overview of Michael's background and explained that Michael "was born without many of the advantages many of us have known," but unlike the cases that used a social worker or other expert to explain why such factors placed the defendant at greater risk for violent behavior, the defense in this case left Michael's history to stand on its own without explaining why such evidence would be relevant for understanding his decisions later in life. This does not mean that Michael's defense attorneys were not attempting to subvert hegemonic individualism. They appeared to be trying; they just lacked the evidence to do so. For example, in the summation, one of the defense attorneys noted that Michael:

> was raised in an abusive home, no positive role model, and he was abandoned as a teenager. Many of us could never fathom that. We could never imagine being locked in a closet while your mother or your father were outside drinking and partying and whatever else they're doing in a room. It's just unimaginable that you could do that to a child.

So, Michael's attorneys did try to contextualize his actions as rooted in a more complex story of structural deprivation, but without any expert testimony, there was no explanation for how these experiences affected Michael. Many people experience, as the defense attorney put it, "a tough family life" without "enjoying all of the things that you and I and many other people do." Most of them do not commit murder. The defense did try to point out that the defendant's choices were not entirely his own. They noted that he was abandoned as a teenager and that the only people with whom he was left to affiliate were "the ones on the street." With only second-hand knowledge of family members who were half a country away when these events were occurring and without providing any sociological data on the ill effects of these risk factors, the defense failed to provide jurors with any understanding of why evidence of the dangerous environment in which Michael had grown up would even be relevant for understanding why he killed. Thus, the defense failed to fully contextualize Michael's behavior. Because this is a study of mitigation at trial and not of the investigation and collection of mitigating evidence, it is unknown if this lack of evidence was a result of poor investigatory efforts on the part of defense counsel or the result of the evidence simply not existing. After all, not all cases are equally mitigated. Some defendants simply have less structural mitigation in their life histories or do not have any good record of their past experiences and therefore do not provide the attorneys with an opportunity to challenge the cultural master narrative.

Humanizing Defendants' Relationships

The final defense strategy was to try to humanize the defendant by showing him embedded in a web of social relationships. This was another effort to contextualize the defendants by showing that they are capable of both good and bad deeds; they are not just inherently "bad guys." Rather, depending on the context, they are capable of very positive feats and they therefore should not be defined solely by the worst thing they have ever done. This was an attempt to show the murder as an anomaly in a life characterized by lawful behavior that positively impacts others and an attempt to show that the defendant matters to other people and that his execution would not just affect the condemned killer—it would affect all who love him. This attempt to draw social connections between the defendant and his loved ones offers a challenge to the culture of rugged individualism in which people are solely responsible for themselves, have no emotional ties to others, and only kill because they are inherently bad people bent on death and destruction (Scheingold, 1984).

The defense attempts at humanization occurred in all eight trials, and it usually involved showing how the defendant's execution would negatively impact his friends or family—particularly any children he may have had. In fact, all eight mitigation cases involved a family member of the defendant testifying about how much he or she would be devastated by the defendant's execution, which was designed to show the jury and judge that someone other than the defendant would be affected by his execution, that he was loved, that he is embedded in a web of familial and social relationships that are distinctly human, and that an execution would simply create more innocent victims. As Sundby notes, testimony from the defendant's family and friends helps show the jury "that someone cares about the defendant and believes that he has some redeeming value" and "that there is good in the defendant, as well as evil" (1997, pp. 1152-3). Sundby (1997) says such testimony usually impacts the jury emotionally and allows jurors to relate to someone who will be affected by the execution in a way they cannot relate to the defendant.

The typical family member testified as to the defendant's positive qualities, all the good things he has done, how much they all love him (and why), and the positive impact the defendant could still have on his family if he were allowed to live. They normally explained that the family would continue to visit the defendant, and when asked what impact the defendant's execution would have on the family, the typical answer was, "Devastating," or something similar. Donald's mother responded, "I won't know what to do. I'll probably kill myself, you know?" Jerry's mother broke down crying: "Well, he just can't be, that's all … (witness crying) …" (ellipsis in original), and Ted's mother begged the jury, "Please, please, please, don't kill my son." In most of the cases, a family member was also used to show the jury pictures of the defendant as a child in an attempt to show jurors that the defendant was not always the murderer that he is now; he was a person with a childhood and a family just like everyone else. Many described the good times they had with the defendant or the positive impact he had on his family while he was around, also trying to show that the defendant is capable of both good and bad; he is not inherently bad.

When the defendant had children, his fatherhood and his children's innocence were exploited in the defense's attempt to humanize the defendant. After all, what could better illustrate the positive aspects of the defendant? Parenthood is the antithesis of killing. The message is clear: "Perhaps the defendant made a mistake and is guilty of murder, but he also helped to create, care for, and nurture a new life, so he cannot be all bad. If he was all bad, how did he create this little miracle? Perhaps there is some redeeming quality in the defendant." The negative impact of an execution on the defendant's children was also exploited as a reason to spare the defendant, but it also helped to contextualize the defendant and show that he could be seen in different lights. To the victim's family, he may be an evil piece of trash worthy of death, but to the defendant's family, he is a loving son, brother, and father. As Steve's attorney put it in his opening statement:

> And we will argue that his execution will be a tragedy of [*sic*: for] his family and especially four year old daughter, which affection she still receives even though he is still in jail. In other words, his execution will serve to inflict pain on other innocent people who love him, count on him, and even though he is in jail, still have contact with him.

Steve even mentioned his children in his allocution and asked that his life be spared

> so that my loved ones can continue to visit me and that I may continue to have some part in the upbringing of my kids, so I may show them right from wrong, show them the mistakes that I've made in my life that led me to be where I am today.

In summation, Steve's attorney mentioned that he "does and still can have value as a human being …" because he "plays an important role to certain people in their lives."

The same strategy is evident in every case in which the defendant was a father. Donald's defense team, for example, told the jurors that Donald had a young son who "visits him every week in prison" and who would be harmed by his execution. They told the jury that the boy's mother and Donald's mother and grandmother would all be negatively impacted by the defendant's death; all three testified as such in the penalty trial. Donald even addressed the court and asked the judge to spare his life so he could have some involvement in his son's life. The defense attorney argued in his closing that the Donald's son was, "Probably the most innocent person other than the [victim's] family in all of this tragedy …" In Alan's trial, the defense argued that by killing Alan, his "children would be without a father," and "a loving family … will be devastated." He told the jury that Alan "viewed himself as responsible for three children" and that Alan, therefore, had

"Value as a human being ..." Jerry's jury was told that if he was allowed to live, "he will be able to remain in contact with his children ..." In the closing, one of the defense attorneys mentioned that an execution would affect his children and asked, "Has he no redeeming acts ... as a father?" Charlie was described by one of his lawyers as "a good father, even in prison ..." He told the judge and jury that Charlie's daughter's mother

> wants him to have a role in his daughter and her daughter's life because he had a role in her life when he was out on the streets. And she recognizes him as daddy, and she goes down there and still sees him, and she would like to have that for her daughter.

He then made the argument that executing the defendant "would just continue to make additional victims: [Charlie]'s daughters, his family." In his allocution, Charlie mentioned the ordeal through which his children, his wife, and his mother were going, and in the summation, the defense said that Charlie's "family still supports him," that he maintains relationships with them, and that killing him will leave two children without a father.

Conclusion

The findings in this chapter reveal a substantially more complex process than predicted by Dunn and Kaplan's (2009) theory of hegemonic individualism. They reveal that, as suggested by Ewick and Silbey (1995), the stories told in mitigation have the power both to support hegemonic narratives and to subvert them. It appears that most defense lawyers were trying to offer stories that challenged the taken-for-granted beliefs about individual responsibility and constructing defenses that helped to educate jurors about the impact past experiences have on one's decisions and behaviors in the present. Utilizing evidence derived from the defendant's life history, five defense teams used expert testimony to present contextualizing mitigation that placed at least some of the blame for the defendants' actions on factors beyond their control; a sixth case involved an attempt to discuss factors beyond the defendant's control but did not utilize an expert to make this connection explicit. Rather than relying solely on the "psy-complex" that professionalizes individual explanations, as Dunn and Kaplan (2009) feared, the defense lawyers in these six cases did try to challenge the hegemonic story that justifies the death penalty in the first place. Furthermore, in all eight trials, defense counsel attempted to humanize their clients by placing them within a web of social relationships in which they were capable of loving and being loved, of doing positive things, and being missed if they were to be executed. These efforts tried to connect the defendants to the larger social world and show how what happens to them can affect other people and that they are not inherently and universally bad—they are also capable of doing many positive things.

This conclusion suggests that mitigation is a nuanced process that is at times able to challenge the cultural master narrative. Defense attorneys do not just focus on defendants' individual agency or personal characteristics, and they do not rely solely upon de-contextualizing discourses. Rather they typically interweave individualistic tales with contextualizing ones that attempt to show the influence of *external* social forces on their clients' behaviors. In other words, robust attempts were made by attorneys and mitigation experts to challenge the prevailing theory that everyone has the same opportunity and everyone becomes whatever they freely choose. They tried to demonstrate the ways in which defendants' choices were constrained and that even though they chose to commit crime, they did so for a plethora of reasons beyond their control. Furthermore, in all eight cases, defense attorneys also tried to humanize the defendants by having their families testify and discussing the impact on these people if the defendants were executed or spared. This was an effort to embed the defendants within a web of social and familial relationships and to show that defendants are not islands unto themselves. They are not evil killers bent on destruction with no conceivable human emotion. They love and can be loved just like everyone else; therefore, they are capable of making mistakes just like everyone else. They are also capable of good, not just the evil acts that brought them to the attention of the judge and jury.

It is important to note, however, that despite the attempts to contextualize and humanize the defendants' behaviors and despite the fact that all five cases that used the testimony of an expert witness to present contextualizing mitigation involved minority defendants, not a single mention of racial inequality appeared in the transcripts. In fact, race was so overlooked that it was impossible to determine the defendants' or victims' races from the transcripts. Granted, the ruling in *McCleskey v. Kemp* (1987) certainly makes the use of racial discrimination-based arguments more challenging in capital cases, but since racial inequality is a fundamental feature of the death sentencing process and in the distribution of structural mitigation (Haney, 2004), it is imperative that capital defense attorneys find ways to address the issue (Lyon, 2004). By ignoring the issue, capital defense attorneys may actually be inadvertently supporting another hegemonic story that is a variant of psychological individualism: color-blindness. In this view, Civil Rights legislation of the 1960s was enough to ensure racial equality and no steps need to be taken to address persistent racial differences in educational outcomes, economic standings, or criminal justice processing. It is virtually impossible to give a truly contextualizing account of a minority defendant's life without addressing the insidious forms of subtle, institutionalized, structural forms of racism that infect their daily lives but about which (predominantly) white capital jurors are often ignorant and with which they are typically incapable of empathizing (Haney, 2004).

Yet, none of the cases in this sample offered the decision makers with any opportunity to grapple with the tremendous differences between being white and non-white in a society that privileges whiteness or to appreciate how those differences affect personality formation, life opportunities, and behavior. Because jurors and judges are situated so differently than the defendants over whom they sit in judgment and are unlikely to have any direct experience with structural racism, concentrated disadvantage, or unsafe neighborhoods and homes, they struggle to empathize with the defendants' plights, to understand how these factors affected them, or to appreciate the significance of their life histories. Getting jurors to bridge this empathetic divide "requires special attention to the nature of the institutions into which [capital defendants] are disproportionately drawn" (Haney, 2004, p. 1565). Lyon (2004) has argued that there are ways to make jurors viscerally aware of the substantial social distance between themselves and the defendants and the vast difference between their hardships and the hardships faced by typical capital defendants, even when race is not a salient issue in the trial, and that it is imperative that capital defense attorneys present such evidence. Unfortunately, none of the attorneys in these eight cases made any efforts to educate the jurors about the different social worlds in which most minorities reside, a fact that perpetuates the color-blind racism that simultaneously causes minorities to be more likely to live in conditions that are conducive to capital violence and to be devalued (as both victims and offenders) by the criminal justice system.

Chapter 4
"You Still Don't Kill Somebody": Hegemonic Individualism and Jurors' Sentencing Recommendations

> "If I felt he intentionally went out to kill somebody … I would have voted for the death penalty."

> "… I understand that it's possible to have someone die without you wanting that to happen or planning that to happen, but that wasn't what happened here"

> "… we're all born with equal opportunities and equal choices, just whether or not we choose to act on good choices …"

In Chapter 3, it was demonstrated that in some cases, defense attorneys were at least attempting to contextualize their clients' behaviors, but this does not answer how juries or judges understand or respond to these stories. The Supreme Court has ruled that the constitutionality of the death penalty rests on an assumption that sentencers provide "a reasoned moral response" (*California v. Brown*, 1987; *Penry v. Lynaugh*, 1989) and that they consider all relevant evidence (*Eddings v. Oklahoma*, 1982). So, are they? Prior studies of capital juries discussed in Chapter 1 suggest that they are unlikely to consider factors unrelated to the crime, but without an examination of how jurors respond to specific evidence in specific cases, we really do not know. The interviews with 35 jurors from these eight cases, however, show that even when contextualizing stories were told in the mitigation case, jurors were uninterested. No juror recommended a life sentence because of the defendant's past or his social history. Rather, the primary concern of the jurors was with assessing culpability (the question of the guilt stage). If they were satisfied that the defendant intended the death of the victim, they voted for a death sentence; if they harbored doubts as to the defendant's intent, they voted for life. In fact, 60 percent of the jurors in this sample had made up their minds as to the punishment by the conclusion of the guilt trial, most of the jurors claimed to have little or no recall of the life history evidence, even when reminded about it by the interviewer, and those who could recall it either gave it little weight or were outwardly hostile to its presentation. This is true both for jurors who recommended life and those who recommended death. For the jurors in this sample, the death sentencing decision was simple and straightforward: he who intends the death for which he is convicted should be put to death; all others should be spared. The findings of this research are consistent with prior studies on capital juries, but through the use of trial transcripts, this research was able to explore the specific content of what jurors ignore and what they find useful. In this way, these interviews were able to reveal *why* the jurors are so focused on culpability: because they reject the importance of contextual life history evidence even when it is presented to them.

The Question of Intent: How Jurors Decide on Punishment

For 32 of the 35 jurors interviewed in this study, the decision on punishment was based on a simple question: Did the defendant mean to do it? Even when specifically asked about the use of contextualizing mitigation, they claimed not to recall such evidence, claimed such evidence was not relevant to their sentencing decisions, or were outright hostile to such evidence. In other words, even when the defense presented a detailed contextualizing mitigation story, the jurors were unmoved by it, even those who supported a life sentence. The sentencing recommendation came down to a simple question of culpability, the focus of the guilt trial. Jurors' sentencing recommendations, therefore, are not truly bifurcated into a guilt question and a sentencing question. For the jurors, guilt and sentencing were the same thing, and by delaying the presentation of contextualizing mitigation until after the guilt question had been answered, the bifurcated trial, ironically, prevented jurors from considering such evidence (Haney, 2005).

Life Recommendations When Intent is in Doubt

Most of those who recommended a life sentence made it abundantly clear that the rationale for their recommendation was lingering doubt over the defendant's role or intent in the crime. None of them indicated that horrific events in the defendant's past helped them to understand why the defendant did what he did, caused them to empathize with him, or made them less likely to vote for death. In fact, seven of the ten jurors who confirmed voting for a life sentence indicated that they had made up their mind as to the appropriate punishment before the penalty trial even began. An eleventh juror insisted that—despite court records to the contrary—she did not participate in the penalty trial. Based upon her responses, it is most likely that she voted for a life sentence, and her insistence that their verdict did not permit a death sentence and her conviction that she did not serve on the penalty phase both indicate that she was closed off to penalty phase evidence. In the sections that follow, the responses of jurors who voted for life will be presented. Responses will be grouped by trial, and the trials will be discussed in the same order as they were in Chapter 3 to assist with connecting the jurors' answers to the mitigation that was presented at trial.

Donald: "I Can't Tell You Whether He Pulled the Trigger"

The jury from Donald's trial offers an excellent example of the way jurors make their sentencing decisions. Seven jurors recommended a life sentence for

Donald, but despite the use of contextualizing mitigation discussed in Chapter 3, none of the three interviewed jurors who voted for life did so in response to this evidence. On the contrary, they ignored or downplayed the contextual evidence and voted for life based upon the individualizing fact that they doubted Donald's culpability. In fact, one juror was so unconcerned with life history evidence that she convinced herself that no evidence as to the appropriate punishment was even presented and the jury was dismissed following the guilty verdict. She still explained to the interviewer why she opposed a death sentence for Donald: "I definitely didn't think he should be given a death sentence" because "there was no doubt in my mind then [when evidence of the co-perpetrators' involvement was presented] he was not the guilty one." This juror's belief that a co-perpetrator fired the fatal bullet led her to conclude that the defendant did not deserve death, and she made it clear that nothing beyond that question entered into her decision making.

The other two interviewed jurors who voted for life in Donald's trial demonstrated the same type of reasoning. Although both could recall serving on the penalty trial, neither utilized the contextualizing mitigation to reach their sentencing decision. In fact, Mark was able to recall that Donald presented life history evidence, but he said this evidence was ineffective. On the contrary, Mark was unable to recommend a death sentence because he was not sure whether Donald pulled the trigger:

> In my mind I came to the realization of whether he was the gunman or whether he wasn't, I couldn't tell you that ... Whether he was an accomplice or pulled the trigger, I can't tell you that ... I can't tell you whether he pulled the trigger [so] I can't tell you whether he should get the chair or lethal injection—I'm not sure how Delaware does it. ... I [decided on] life in prison because I still was not convinced [whether] he did not pull the trigger or he did.

This uncertainty was the most helpful factor to Mark for reaching his sentencing recommendation. Mark indicated that the jury did discuss whether someone's marginalized upbringing is relevant, but he said the jury's overall recommendation was "based on the fact that we believed he was associated with it, but we could never—if I remember right—finger him with the gun or determine that he was the person that pulled the trigger."

Tom confirmed this account. After the conclusion of the interview, Tom mentioned in casual conversation with the interviewer that jurors are simply not interested in a defendant's life history. They may consider it interesting, but they do not consider it relevant to their sentencing recommendations. During the interview, Tom claimed to have no recollection of either defense social worker or their testimonies. He also stated, "There really wasn't any specific evidence" that was most helpful to him in reaching his punishment decision "because I came in there knowing that based on our previous verdict on him not necessarily being the one that pulled the trigger that I was not comfortable having a person sentenced to death for that uncertainty. From a moral standpoint I didn't think that was appropriate."

Roger: "I Didn't Think He Planned It"

Roger's jury also recommended a life sentence by a seven-to-five margin, but only one of the jurors who voted for life was interviewed. According to her interview, Kelly supported a life sentence because she had doubts as to Roger's culpability and because she did not believe the crime was heinous enough for a death sentence. In her interview, she had excellent recall of the social worker's testimony in Roger's case and was able to accurately recall Roger's life history. Yet, she indicated that she did not use this evidence in her sentencing decision. When asked specifically if the social worker's testimony had any impact on her decision, she replied, "More about the crime itself." She had made up her mind prior to the penalty phase because, "I just think capital punishment should be reserved for the most heinous crimes, and I just didn't think that was a most heinous crime …" In her words, "I didn't think he planned it. I didn't think he tortured him. It was almost like an accident or something." So even though this juror listened to and processed the defendant's life history and subsequently recommended a life sentence, she did not utilize such evidence in her decision. The reason for her recommendation remained narrowly focused on the defendant's individual responsibility: "I think the lack of evidence was most helpful in making my decision. I just wasn't sure. I was very unsure throughout the whole trial because I wasn't a hundred percent sure that he was guilty of this crime."

Ted: "I Wasn't a Hundred Percent Sure"

Ted's case, the final life case in which contextual mitigation was presented, offers the best illustration of the jurors' preoccupation with culpability because Ted's defense offered numerous examples of abuse and neglect that Ted experienced throughout his most formative years and there were four jurors interviewed who voted for a life sentence. Yet, *none* of them could accurately recall the facts of Ted's childhood. In fact, none of the six jurors interviewed from this trial had any recollection of the defense's psychologist and only Rachel recalled the forensic nurse, but she gave her testimony no credibility:

> Actually there was also a nurse … and I had to say … [the nurse's] testimony was very far-fetched and I think [the nurse] realized that … [the nurse] really stretched the truth big time. I had to almost contain myself sometimes with the medical testimony of the so-called expert witnesses 'cause they'll ask them too how much are you getting paid to testify—the opposite lawyer will ask. So they have to admit and I just wanted to burst out laughing, "My God, I could have said what you said 'cause it's all like fabricated." So yeah it didn't do them a justice … [The nurse's] testimony was really stretching it.

Sundby (1997) identified the same reaction among his sample of California capital jurors. According to Sundby (1997), jurors are highly skeptical of defense experts. They perceive them to be "hired guns" who do not accurately describe human behavior, so rather than defer to their expertise, jurors will often tune out these experts. In light of these findings, it is perhaps not surprising that none of the jurors could recall (or chose not to divulge) a single detail of Ted's upbringing.

Rather than basing their sentencing recommendations on the contextualizing mitigating evidence Ted presented in the penalty phase, the four jurors who supported a life sentence appeared to base their decisions on doubts they harbored over Ted's intent—the guilt-phase question. In the words of Shannon:

> I just did not believe that he went there to intentionally kill him. I know he went there to rob him. I couldn't give somebody a death penalty if I wasn't absolutely one hundred percent sure that he went there with the intentions of killing him. I wasn't a hundred percent sure, and nothing could change my mind.

Shannon also indicated that the primary discussion during the punishment deliberations focused on Ted's criminal intent, and Rachel corroborated this account by conceding that the jury "had decided early on that it was not premeditated" and indicated that the jury felt that since they did not believe the murder was premeditated and "didn't get the impression that he was a hardened criminal," they "really should not put him to death." Pam and Matt, the remaining life supporters included in the sample, also confirmed these observations. Pam stated that during the guilt trial the jury "had come to the decision that he didn't plan to kill him so that it shouldn't be a death penalty," and Matt indicated:

> Most of the jurors, myself included, thought that yes, he was responsible for killing this person, but we didn't feel like it was a premeditated "I'm gonna walk up and just shoot the person," so most of us had the feeling that yes, he should go to jail for it, but no, he should not get the death penalty.

Throughout the interview, Matt indicated his belief that the murder was neither intentional nor planned, and when asked if he would have favored a death sentence if he thought the killing was intentional, he replied affirmatively. Matt indicated that the single most important factor in the jury's punishment decision was how intentional the killing was, and when asked why the defendant's intent was so important to him in making his punishment recommendation, he stated,

> Because *if I felt he intentionally went out to kill somebody, personally speaking. I would have voted for the death penalty,* but it's hard for me to put somebody—be the person that votes to put somebody to death when I'm not necessarily convinced that that was what they were intending to do from the beginning. (emphasis added)

Death Recommendations When There is No Doubt

This culpability-based reasoning may not sound problematic among jurors who recommended a life sentence. After all, if they felt the defendant was simply not culpable enough to deserve a death sentence, there may have been no need to analyze the evidence any further. However, Matt's indication that he would have voted for death if he felt the killing was intentional suggests he would not have been swayed by any array of mitigating circumstances. When looking at those jurors who did decide the defendant intended death, it is clear that they too ended their analysis at this point and decided that death was the appropriate sentence without giving consideration to mitigation. In other words, the decision-making processes demonstrated by the jurors who recommended life are more pronounced, and far more concerning, among the jurors who voted for death.

This section will first present the rationales used by the jurors in Steve's and Charlie's cases since they are the two defendants sentenced to death who presented contextualizing life history evidence with the assistance of expert mitigation testimony. In neither case, however, was such evidence considered by jurors in their sentencing recommendations. This section then proceeds to consider the thought processes of jurors in Michael's and Jerry's trials. Although neither defendant presented any expert testimony to contextualize their behaviors, the responses of the jurors suggest that even if such evidence was presented, they would not have considered it. Lastly, this section considers the highly illuminating responses of jurors who voted for death on the life cases. Being forced to confront majorities who opposed them, the responses of these men and women indicate how strongly they relied upon commonsense conceptions of individual responsibility in their resistance to a life sentence.

Steve: "He was Guilty"

Steve's jury recommended death by a vote of nine-to-three. Despite the presentation of the contextualizing evidence discussed in Chapter 3, none of the three jurors who were interviewed could recall the mitigation experts, and only Larry could even recall Steve's upbringing being part of the mitigation case, but he described the life history evidence as an excuse: "The defense said it wasn't really his fault. It was his upbringing, the kind of life he lived and painted it as somebody else's issue. He just happened to be in a bad circumstance." Larry also made it clear that none of this evidence factored into his sentencing decision. According to Larry, the most important factor to the jury was Steve's "repetitiveness in the same type of crimes," and the evidence that was most useful for Larry personally was "the testimony of the repetitiveness and the callousness" of the defendant's actions.

James took a similar approach. He indicated that "the nature of the crime" was the most helpful evidence to him, that the three jurors who opposed a death sentence were concerned that Steve may not have done it, and that the jurors who supported a death sentence argued, "That basically he was guilty." In fact,

Brittany even said, "We pretty well decided most of it during the first [phase]," which implies that the jury were only concerned with the defendant's level of guilt, regardless of his terrible childhood experiences or the undue influence the co-perpetrator had on his behavior—evidence that would not have been presented until after the jury had already made up its mind.

Charlie: "When It Became Obvious He was the Guy"

Charlie's jury unanimously recommended a death sentence—perhaps not surprising considering the death of the young child. However, neither juror who was interviewed took Charlie's life history into account. Both indicated recalling Charlie's life history when specifically asked about the defense experts, but this evidence did not find its way into the jurors' weighing process. According to Frank, he knew that Charlie deserved a death sentence "When it became obvious he was the guy that committed what I felt was a cold-blooded killing … [because I] felt he had done it mercilessly with no remorse." John explained that the "the nail in the coffin" was when "[the defendant's] brother could not corroborate the defense's position [at the guilt stage]" because the defendant's innocence claim "didn't make sense." Neither of these interviews suggests that these jurors considered or weighed any of the contextual factors that they recalled from the penalty phase. In fact, in both instances, they had decided the defendant was unfit to live based solely on guilt phase evidence; the presented life history evidence did not even get considered in their decisions. This is not a case where the jurors considered contextual mitigation but decided the callousness of the offense outweighed such factors; they made up their minds before even being presented with such evidence and did not give any consideration to the potentially mitigating effects of Charlie's prior experiences.

Michael: "A Pretty Vicious, Cold Person"

As described in Chapter 3, Michael's defense utilized no expert witnesses, but they did attempt to offer some contextualization through the testimony of his father and an aunt. Although they did not use any expert testimony, they did give the jurors some opportunity to see the influence of factors beyond Michael's control. Yet, none of the three jurors who were interviewed gave any weight to the life history evidence, and their reason for giving it no weight had nothing to do with the lack of expert testimony or the evidence's questionable credibility (coming from second-hand accounts of family members). Rather, they gave it no consideration because it was not related to the crime. According to Janine, the jury's punishment deliberations focused on whether Michael or his co-perpetrator fired the fatal shot, and the evidence that was most useful to her was "the manner in which the crime was committed." Janine was "absolutely convinced" that Michael deserved a death sentence at the conclusion of the guilt phase because the closing arguments at the guilt stage did away with any doubts she still harbored over Michael's guilt.

In describing her punishment decision, she said, "I would have to say I just felt he was there, did the crime, and it was needless and brutal."

Daniel's answers verify Janine's account. According to Daniel, the most important factors in the jury's sentencing decision were "his whole role and how the murder was committed. It was very unnecessary. It was done in such a cold blooded way." Later, Daniel was asked what evidence or testimony was most helpful in reaching his own punishment decision, which led to the following exchange:

> Daniel: I think just the testimony of what exactly happened and how it happened, mostly from [the victim's widow] who was there and the forensic evidence that was presented to back that up.
>
> Interviewer: Why was this most helpful to you?
>
> Daniel: It really gave me a clear picture of what the two people who committed this crime, again how cold blooded and vicious it was. It was pretty cut and dried as far as the actual events that happened and how it happened.

As in the two death cases in which the defense used expert testimony to present contextual life history, the jurors from this case utilized evidence of the defendant's culpability as their sole or primary sentencing rationale. The only part of the defendant's background that was considered was his criminal history, which contributed to Daniel's conclusion that, "[Michael] was a pretty vicious, cold person in my mind. He had that propensity. People's lives, that if he had the chance, I think he—that he didn't care about others [and] would have done it again."

Jerry: "He Thought This Out"

Although Jerry's mitigation case did not involve any contextualizing evidence, the responses of the five jurors interviewed from his trial still illuminate the overwhelming focus of jurors on guilt-stage questions in determining sentence. Their responses suggest that even if such evidence was available, it would not have made an impact on the sentencing jury. In the words of Andrea, who decided Jerry deserved a death sentence when the jury reached its guilty verdict, "I think about crimes of passion sometimes, but they're a lot of times done in the heat of a moment, and I don't feel that was the way with him. I think he thought this out and became very self absorbed in what he wanted ..." Sam described the crime as "cold and calculating, and he knew what he wanted to do," later explaining that Jerry "thought long and hard about his situation and where he wanted to be and then he came up with this plan. So to me it was cold and calculated." The jurors most in favor of a death sentence, according to Sam's recollections, stressed "the cold, calculated way he perpetrated the crime." Robert explained, "From what I knew of courts, I knew what elements they were going to be in order to get a death penalty, and I knew already that the guilt part had brought out all those elements, so I was pretty convinced he met all the criteria for the death penalty." Robert, therefore, was completely closed off to whatever evidence Jerry may have presented in mitigation. Such evidence was completely irrelevant to Robert, who was "absolutely convinced" that Jerry deserved a death sentence by the time the guilt stage ended. When asked what evidence convinced him Jerry deserved to die, he stated, "The actual murder, the weapon being found, the fact that it was done for the money for the insurance policy …" In other words, the evidence that convinced him that Jerry was guilty and did it for money—all guilt-stage evidence—also convinced him Jerry should be executed. Even if the defense had a strong mitigation case to present, it would not have mattered to Robert because such facts had not yet been presented when he concluded death was the appropriate sentence.

"This Wasn't a Mistake": Resistance Among Death Supporters on Life Cases

The interviews with numerous death supporters who served on cases with life majorities are instructive as to the jurors' preoccupations with culpability. Their arguments and disagreements centered on how much guilt to attribute to the defendant rather than on how much weight to give the mitigating evidence. If all the evidence was truly being considered, one might expect disagreements over the relative importance to attribute to background factors like abuse, neglect, poverty, and the like. Yet, what the interviews reveal is debate over the defendants' roles or intentions.

For example, Patricia explained that during punishment deliberations the jury debated how much responsibility fell on Ted relative to his co-perpetrators and that the most helpful evidence to her in reaching a sentencing recommendation was how the forensic evidence supported the co-conspirators' testimonies that Ted was the triggerman. She justified her death vote by stating that she "was pretty convinced that he would kill again." Eric also said that he focused on culpability, indicating that the use of a gun in the commission of a robbery implied Ted intended to use it:

> Interviewer: Why did you think [Ted deserved a death sentence at the conclusion of guilt trial but before penalty trial started]?
>
> Eric: Because I understand that it's possible to have someone die without you wanting that to happen or planning that to happen, but that wasn't what happened here. [Ted] *deliberately* brought a gun and [victim] ended up dead.
>
> Interviewer: So because he deliberately brought this gun?
>
> Eric: Yes, and he had to have reason for bringing that. The end of the day, somebody died because of that. (emphasis added)

Similarly, the primary reason given by the five jurors who voted to execute Roger was fear of future dangerousness. In the words of Elliot, a death sentence was justified "because they showed to me that he had no intention … of getting rid of the weapon where he would actually intended to kill again. Otherwise, he would have ditched the firearm and conceal[ed] it, but he went on to commit other crimes." Likewise, Rita voted for a death sentence because "This wasn't just a one-time deal. It made me feel like this wasn't a mistake, that there was a history there, and it was going to go on and on and on." As Elsa put it, she leaned in favor of death "because I think if he was out again he would probably rob somebody else again or rob a store."

Even the jurors who recalled the defense's use of contextualizing mitigation were uninterested in it. Ben, who actually said the only thing he could remember about the penalty phase was Roger's troubled childhood, was only concerned with Roger's future dangerousness: "There would have been more [victims] … If he knew there was anybody else in the house, I believe he would have killed whoever was there." The most helpful evidence to Ben in reaching his sentencing decision was "the fact that if the opportunity presented itself or if the necessity would have presented itself, more people would have been killed." Nicholas had excellent recall of Roger's background, but he did not mention this evidence when he was asked what factors were important to the jury and to his own decision. Nicholas stated that the most important factor in the jury's decision was the fact "that he shot the victim in the back." He also indicated that those in favor of a death sentence argued that the killing was premeditated. To Nicholas, the most important evidence in reaching his own sentencing decision was "what he did and how he did it." If the crime appeared to be more of an accident, Nicholas suggested he may have supported a life sentence, but he concluded that the crime "was just cold and calculating." So, despite recalling Roger's upbringing, neither of these jurors factored it into their sentencing recommendation. Instead, they focused their sentencing decisions entirely on Roger's violent actions: what did he do and how did he do it?

Why Do Jurors Focus on Culpability?

The above discussion provides compelling evidence that jurors' primary (or sole) focus when determining sentence in capital cases is on the guilt-related question of culpability: Did the defendant intend to kill the victim? If the jurors were convinced that he did, they supported a death sentence. The defense's presentation of mitigating life history evidence did not seem to influence these jurors or even get factored into their weighing process, which means they are only focused on factors that are internal to the defendant and that have some direct nexus to the crime. This conclusion was reached in numerous other studies reviewed in Chapter 1. However, the use of trial transcripts allows for an exploration of an important theoretical question: Why are jurors so focused on culpability and uninterested in contextual factors external to the defendant? For the most part, the transcripts destroy the possibility that jurors rely on individualizing factors because that is the only thing with which they are presented. On the contrary, some of these mitigation cases offered extremely contextual structural mitigation, but the jurors still focused on culpability. The interviews and transcripts reveal two possible explanations for the jurors' predominant focus on individualistic evidence: either the power of hegemonic discourses causes them to think of life history evidence as irrelevant, or the prosecutors' efforts to disparage the contextual mitigation as an "excuse" causes them to dismiss such evidence as irrelevant. Either way, the jurors are *not* giving proper consideration to *all* relevant evidence as the Supreme Court expects. Either conclusion is quite troubling because they both suggest that it may not be possible to eliminate the arbitrariness that continues to infect the death sentencing process in America.

Life History is Irrelevant

One possible (and likely) explanation for the jurors' focus on culpability is a strong adherence among jurors to commonsense notions of individual responsibility that causes jurors to distrust or disbelieve evidence that challenges micro-level theories of behavior. Most of the jurors either claimed to be unable to recall the life history evidence that was presented or failed to accurately recall such evidence, even when the interviewer tried priming their memories with information from the trial transcripts. Thus, they would have been unable to utilize such evidence in their sentencing decisions. Yet, even those who accurately recollected the life history evidence outright rejected it as irrelevant. A defendant's social background or upbringing was utilized as a factor in determining sentence by exactly zero jurors, and many jurors were openly hostile to the defendant's presentation of such evidence. To these jurors, as long as there was nothing wrong with the defendant's internal functioning, the factors that may have influenced his decision to be violent were considered extraneous.

As Chelsea from Donald's trial put it, "I felt like [Donald] did it to himself. I would say he's the number one thing. I mean you did it, so you're number one. You're really responsible for yourself." Larry, from Steve's trial, considered Steve's life history a defense ploy to concoct an excuse rather than a mitigating circumstance: "He made [his bad childhood] his mantra, didn't seem to take responsibility. It was always who he was with." As shown above, Larry characterized the mitigation case as, "The defense said it wasn't really his fault." Frank, from Charlie's trial, specifically rejected contextualizing mitigation as irrelevant: "… it can't rub out the incident and it can't eliminate what happened. He may have had some problems, but he still committed the crime, and I think as far as having an impact I don't, I don't recall that that—it didn't have much of an impact on me." John, the other juror interviewed from Charlie's trial, expressed a similar reaction. He noted, "[The defense] did present some background information as to his upbringing and how he found himself in the type of situation he was in, but … *you still don't kill somebody*" (emphasis added).

Elliot's especially hostile reaction to the life history evidence presented in Roger's trial epitomizes the jurors' opposition to considerations of external, environmental influences. As discussed in Chapter 3, Roger's attorneys offered a challenge to hegemonic individualism. They explained that Roger suffered from many experiences in his childhood that were not his fault and that as humans we are predominantly "products of our environment." Elliot was identified by the other jurors as the most influential juror, but he revealed that Roger's use of contextualizing evidence really bothered him:

> Interviewer: Is there anything about this crime that sticks in your mind or that you keep thinking about?
>
> Elliot: That they leveraged his upbringing as part of his defense when I don't particularly agree with that type of defense when *we're all born with equal opportunities and equal choices, just whether or not we choose to act on good choices*, so that bothered me that still entered into the defense. (emphasis added)

Elliot even said that the least effective thing about the defense attorney's performance was trying "to play the sympathy card on the [Roger's] background."

Throughout the interview, Elliot framed Roger's criminality solely as a consequence of personal failings and individual choices by overlooking the existence of a differential opportunity structure and thus constructing an image of a world in which important contextual factors like extreme poverty, an inability to receive a quality education, and early experiences with crime and violence are irrelevant. These responses reflect a "pull yourself up by the bootstraps" mentality that is the hallmark of American individualism. In this account, everyone has equal opportunities and one's life outcome is solely the result of choices the individual has made. Crime and poverty, in this worldview, are not impacted by structural realities; people can simply choose to overcome these disadvantages. Roger, therefore, is just a "bad" person who flubbed his opportunities. In his words, some of the jurors "had issues when we were young but didn't turn out to be criminals." He also argued to the jury, "Everyone has choices as the—as we're put on this earth, and I just didn't feel that [upbringing] was an argument for anyone. I didn't feel it was right. I believe what we needed to look at was the evidence [of the murder]."

Interestingly, the only penalty phase defense witness Elliot could recall was the social worker, but he was hostile to her testimony. When asked what he thought about her testimony, Elliot responded, "That doesn't work well on me because everyone has choices, so it wasn't a good defense for me." Asked if her testimony backfired on the defense, Elliot answered, "Yeah, I would agree with that statement. When someone tries to use someone's upbringing, regardless. Helen Keller, she grew up without hearing or sight and couldn't speak, yet she chose to do a good thing. She could have went another way, but that's her. Disabilities never shut her down." There is quite a bit of irony in this answer. In Elliot's mind (and according to the message of hegemonic individualism) the fact that one person was able to overcome hardships proves everyone should be able to do so. Yet such a story actually distorts the accomplishments of Helen Keller and dehumanizes her while simultaneously supporting an ideology to which she was vehemently opposed (Loewen, 1995). Rather than being the epitome of individualism, as Elliot describes it, the Keller story can be read as a testament to the importance and power of social structural forces. Roger had no equivalent of Anne Sullivan in his life, nor was he blessed with the advantages of race or class. Had Keller been denied such luxuries, she too would have probably been unable to overcome the disadvantages with which she was born. As she put it in her autobiography, "... the power to rise in the world is not within the reach of everyone." She realized that she owed her "success partly to the advantages of [her] birth and environment" (Keller, 1968, p. 156), which led her to become a socialist. Considering the high degree of influence other jurors attributed to Elliot, it follows that this rejection of contextualizing evidence appeared in other interviews. For example, Elsa recalled that Roger had a rough life, "but it just didn't really make a difference that you had a big rough life. A lot of people have a rough life. I'm sure the victim probably had a rough life." Of course, applying this same logic to smoking would imply that cigarettes do not cause cancer because some people who smoke do not develop cancer.

Overall, the accounts repeated in this section offer a compelling theoretical explanation for the consistent findings that capital jurors are obsessed with culpability: American culture teaches them that external social forces do not matter. It is not just that jurors give more weight to elements of the crime in their sentencing decisions, nor is it that defense attorneys fail to contextualize. By specifically asking the jurors about the mitigating evidence presented in the trial, this research finds that the jurors in this research either ignored or were hostile to contextualizing structural mitigation because they denied its causal relevance.

Prosecutorial Disparagement of Mitigation

While it seems likely that the influence of hegemonic individualism causes jurors to reject the relevance of life history evidence, the transcripts reveal another possible explanation for this finding. The prosecutors in the five cases that used mitigation experts to present contextualizing mitigation made forceful attempts to get jurors to dismiss the relevance of such evidence by casting it as an "excuse," so perhaps jurors are not beholden to hegemonic individualism but are simply responding to the prosecutors' deliberate efforts to get them not to consider evidence that the Supreme Court has explicitly stated must be considered. Or perhaps both forces are at work; maybe the arguments made by the prosecutors help to reassure jurors that they do not have to grapple with the powerful impacts of structural mitigation, can rely on their commonsense beliefs, and can reject the relevance of evidence not directly related to the crime.

For example, in his closing argument, the prosecutor in Donald's case argued:

> There comes a time, ladies and gentlemen, in everyone's life when a person accepts responsibility for their actions. The defendant has not accepted any responsibility for any of his acts. We heard about that yesterday [when the mitigating evidence was presented].
>
> We heard that the defendant was a violent criminal, but it was because of his upbringing. It is because of factors beyond his control. He wants you to blame his mother, his father, the neighborhood which he was brought up in, the Addams Family house, and the people that he hung around with.
>
> … Society at some point must say, you are a bad person.

This sounds quite similar to the reasoning used by juror Chelsea: "You're really responsible for yourself."

In fact, in Roger's trial, the prosecution went as far as to argue during its closing, "Defendant's dysfunctional upbringing does not necessarily correlate to mitigation." After all, Roger still made choices according to the prosecution. The prosecution then used the fact that Roger's own mother abstained from crime in an attempt to disprove external causal theories of crime:

> Does that make any sense to you, when this particular scientist [expert witness] has had the opportunity to apply that particular science, … his mother, who's in a far worse situation, she's—she explained to you she had—she herself had been beaten, she herself hated every community she lived in, she was the sibling to all these people involved in drugs and crime, she was in a single-parent home which was completely overcrowded, she was the one who suffered the difficult child bearing, she was the one who dropped out of school and had no formal education after 16, but she didn't turn out the same way.

At one point while discussing the life history evidence, the prosecutor stated that only "children have less of an ability to control their behavior … As they get older, they are expected to conform their behavior more to the behavior of an adult," as if one should be able to forget a lifetime of socialization experiences, subcultural reinforcements, and social pressures the moment one becomes an adult. The logic presented here—that the ability of a few people to overcome hardships proves that social structure is irrelevant and anyone can achieve success if they try hard enough—was repeated by Elliot, who argued that since Helen Keller overcame her disabilities and many jurors "had issues when we were young but didn't turn out to be criminals," Roger should have been able to overcome his disadvantages and avoid crime as well.

Similarly, the prosecution in Ted's trial pointed to those who overcame their disadvantages to convince the jury that they should not give any weight to the environmental forces that affected Ted:

> The defendant made choices. The defendant chose to commit a robbery. …
>
> His sister, [name omitted], made choices. She lived in the same household that the defendant did. And she made choices. She made a choice to become a productive citizen, to go to school, educate herself, to provide for her family. Those were her choices.
>
> You heard from [name omitted] who was in the house a short period of time, but was in that family, and he made choices. He chose to educate himself. He chose to provide for his family.
>
> The defendant didn't make those choices.
>
> The defendant chose to be defined by his life experiences and chose not to make a better life for himself.
>
> …
>
> [Name omitted], his older brother, tried to guide him, to be the role model for him, to be a father figure for him.
>
> And yet, the defendant still made choices.
>
> He chose not to participate in school. He chose to get a life marked by substance abuse and selling drugs.

The prosecutor even contrasted Ted to his victim, whom the prosecutor described as "able to overcome his learning disability. He was slow. He had problems learning. And, yet, his choice was to overcome these obstacles. To be a responsible person. To get a job. To financially provide for his own family. To work hard." This argument, of course, overlooks the substantial differences between Ted and his family members (e.g., being the youngest, being left on his father's porch, spending nights on the street beginning at age 11 due to cramped space, being treated like an unwanted child), but it is designed to get jurors to reject the relevance of social structural forces by pointing to people in very similar situations who had different outcomes. This is precisely what the findings reviewed above indicate the jurors did. The power of prosecutors to influence the decision making of juries can be shown through the responses of Eric, who stated, "[Ted] deliberately brought a gun and [victim] ended up dead. … and he had to have reason for bringing that." This mirrors the prosecutor's closing argument very closely: "And, ultimately, he made choice, to bring a gun to this robbery, shoot the gun, causing [victim]'s death."

In the death cases, too, the language of the jurors who rejected life history evidence seemed to mirror the language of the prosecuting attorneys. During the penalty phase closing arguments, the prosecutors portrayed Steve's mitigation case as an excuse, rather than the explanation that it was supposed to be: "[A]lthough [the defense social worker] never said that she was trying to excuse the murders, what was your read on what she was really saying? … [T]hat is an attempt to excuse what he has done and we submit you should reject that attempt for exactly what it is." In the penalty phase rebuttal closing, the prosecution went on to suggest to the jury that they should not even consider the defendant's life history: "You can't just say, oh, well, the prior murder's important, but, you know, what's really important is risk factors." Later in the rebuttal, he asked the jury if they thought the risk factors meant anything to the victims or their families, and therefore, "they shouldn't mean a thing to you." As shown by Larry's interview, the jurors often parroted this line of thinking: "He made [his bad childhood] his mantra, didn't seem to take responsibility."

The prosecutors in Charlie's trial also referred to his mitigation case as "excuse-making" and argued that Charlie "made choices. He decided to live that violent street life. … [He] made his choices, and he chose to kill." Repeatedly, they referred to Charlie and the crime as "cold and calculated." As the interviews reveal, jurors again adopted similar language. Frank stated, "He may have had some problems, but he still committed the crime …" John also adopted the same logic used by the prosecution: "[The defense] did present some background information … but … *you still don't kill somebody*" (emphasis added).

This reading of the transcripts suggests that jurors may not be completely deaf to sentencing stage evidence and may not be reaching their decisions because of hegemonic individualism. Yet, if they are open to penalty phase evidence, why did none of the jurors adopt the defense's view of the evidence and indicate that they opposed a death sentence because of factors beyond the defendant's control that contributed to his conduct—or at the very least indicate that they considered such an explanation in their decision? Why did they adopt the language used by prosecutors and not defenders? Although a single study of eight mitigation cases cannot answer this question definitively, a likely explanation is that the prosecutors' attempts to disparage structural mitigation comported more closely with the jurors' already existing worldview and so it was easier for them to relate to and identify with these arguments. Thus, the prosecutors may have been easing the tension wrought by the defense's theories of behavior that challenged the jurors' pre-existing beliefs and may have helped to reassure the jurors that their way of thinking about the world is acceptable. They do not have to deal with understanding "a social world of events governed by causes beyond human control" (Sarat, 1995, p. 1129) or the "sociocultural aspects of being human" (Dunn & Kaplan, 2009, p. 364) if they do not want to. The ability of humans to make a choice is all that matters in this account. The fact that those choices are going to be influenced, constrained, or enabled by economic, historical, political, and social forces over which the actor has absolutely no control is of no consequence.

A Note on Humanizing Evidence

The astute reader will have noticed that the jurors from Alan's trial have yet to be discussed. This is because his case represents a bit of an outlier for this sample. He did not present *any* evidence pertaining to his past, but his jury also did not base their 11-1 life recommendation on doubts they harbored over his culpability like the juries in the other three life cases did. On the contrary, they voted for life because they came to recognize Alan's humanity, which tripped their moral prohibitions against killing. It is not clear why the jurors in Alan's trial came to focus on his humanity while the jurors in the other trials focused on culpability. This is not to say that other jurors did not come to recognize the humanity of their defendants. In fact, as will be shown below and as predicted by Sundby (1997), many jurors responded well to the defense attorneys' efforts to humanize their clients. However, with the exception of the jurors on Alan's trial, the *primary* sentencing rationale espoused by the jurors was the defendant's criminal intent. This, too, would be predicted by Sundby's (1997) findings. Family members and friends may be able to humanize defendants but because jurors believe that these witnesses have a bias in favor of the defendant, jurors tend to see such evidence "as a defense ploy to play upon their emotions" and therefore attach less credibility to it (Sundby, 1997, p. 1163).

Nevertheless, the three jurors who were interviewed from Alan's trial who voted for life discussed the ways an execution would affect Alan's family and children and how he did not fit their typical image of a killer. In a way, this contextualizes Alan by placing him within a web of social relationships, but it does not offer a contextualized image of Alan's behavior. In the words of Diane, "… his parent[s] had nothing to do with the crime so why punish the parents?" Diane said that the most helpful evidence in reaching her sentencing decision was the defendant's age and family. She went on to explain, "I had boys the same age, and boys make major mistakes in life, and I think he just made a major mistake and thought he needed to sit and think about it." By referring to the murder as a "mistake," Diane implies that she had an understanding of social context and utilized it in reaching a sentencing decision. This is the only juror in the entire sample who even hinted at context as reason for his or her recommendation, but since no life history evidence was presented in Alan's case, she could not make a full accounting of social context, so the reference is only implied. When asked what evidence was *most* helpful to her in reaching her sentencing decision, Diane stated, "I guess it would be his age and his family." Stacey also focused on Alan's family, stating, "His family was there. His mother was there, and I was—I almost could put myself in her place. I think as long as he wasn't back on the street, she wouldn't lose him completely." Justin even noted that the main reason the defense gave for sparing Alan was that he had "a daughter or son, and it would be a shame if that child grew up without a father; that was the big thing." The lone death supporter on Alan's jury even noted that Alan appeared "like a normal person, did not appear as a vicious type of individual just from looking at him."

Jurors in other cases also made humanizing comments about the defendant or discussed the impact an execution would have on his family or children. As mentioned, *none* of them used this as their primary sentencing rationale, but it is clear that such considerations did make their way into the decision-making processes of at least some jurors. Pam, who voted for life in Ted's trial, stated, "You're always affected by the [defendant's] mother. She's pleading for his life and you feel sorry for her …" Matt also indicated that Ted's mother was a particularly effective witness "because I thought you could tell she was obviously somebody who cared a great deal about her son, obviously, and … she just didn't want to see him killed …" He later said that Ted's mother "reminded me of my mother. Just the fact that you could tell that even though he did something really awful, she cared about him enough to be there by his side every day." Rachel, on the other hand, humanized Ted by focusing on his appearance and demeanor: "He presented as being clean and neat. He just looked like an average person, didn't look like a street person or a drug addict … He didn't look like a hardened criminal with a long rap sheet or whatever." A similar line was used by Kelly, who voted for life in Roger's trial: "He didn't seem like a vicious person … I saw him cry a lot in the courtroom." She later stated, "I felt very sorry for him; I thought he was just a scared kid."

Even death voters seemed to consider the testimony of family members—even when they rejected life history evidence. Both death voters interviewed from Ted's trial stated that the most effective defense evidence came from family members, and Ben, who voted for a death sentence in Roger's trial stated the family testimony was "effective because I'm compassionate. That kind of stuff hits home with me. I always try to give people the benefit of the doubt in just about every situation I run across. … I didn't want to see any more pain spread around to any more people …" Nicholas, who also voted for death in Roger's trial even went as far as to say that Roger reminded him of his own son: "I could constantly see myself end[ing] up being in the same situation with my son in trouble." Elsa echoed these sentiments, stating that Roger "seemed like a regular boy. He looked like he could have been my son." Brittany, who supported a death sentence for Steve, indicated that concern for Steve's daughter did play a part in her sentencing recommendation and did weigh against a death sentence: "If we put [Steve] in jail, she's still gonna have a father, but if we sentence him to death then she won't have a father, so could somebody actually take a father away from a daughter?" Brittany later said the defense's strongest argument for a life sentence was "because he had a daughter."

Conclusion

Dunn and Kaplan ask, "Are there tools outside the psy-complex that could be used to avoid death sentences while simultaneously combating destructive individualism" (2009, p. 363)? From the responses of these 35 capital jurors, the answer to that question appears to be "No." The jurors appear to reject challenges to individualism. Their sentencing decisions reflect an individualistic interpretation of the world and of human behavior. Even when the defense offered contextualizing evidence, the jurors were preoccupied with culpability and, in some cases, were downright hostile to contextualizing explanations. This conclusion reveals a troubling possibility: that hegemonic individualism prevents most jurors from considering contextualizing mitigation derived from environmental influences. These findings are not definitive, but this conclusion is strongly supported by the data presented in this chapter. With the exception of Alan's case, all of the jurors in this sample based their sentencing recommendations predominantly on the defendant's level of culpability. If they were convinced the defendant intended to kill the victim, they voted for death; if they harbored doubts, they voted for life. *None* of the jurors gave any weight to the contextualizing life history evidence; many failed to remember it; and those who did recall it gave it no weight or even treated it negatively. This is not to suggest that capital jurors *never*_consider contextualizing evidence. There are certainly occasional examples of capital jurors in other samples who do consider contextual mitigation, and it is possible that with better orchestration (Sundby 1997), defense attorneys might be able to get jurors to consider life history evidence, but such examples are so rare and the type of orchestration required takes such a Herculean effort by a well-funded and incredibly talented capital defense team that even when there is just the right confluence of circumstances to permit the type of orchestration suggested by Sundby (1997), it happens so rarely as to be wantonly and freakishly random.

It is also important to understand that these findings are *not* a criticism of the 35 men and women who participated in this study. On the contrary, they illuminate the difficulties jurors face. They enter the courtroom with ingrained cultural messages that close them off from contextualizing evidence. This finding indicates the power of hegemonic discourses *and* of the inability of guided discretion statutes to overcome taken-for-granted cultural understandings that are rarely questioned because they are commonsensical. Despite the attempts of the Supreme Court to make the death sentencing process more rational and less arbitrary, cultural discourse teaches Americans that individual responsibility is all that matters, and this impedes the jurors' abilities to consider alternative explanations for behavior. Therefore, it is not the jurors' faults that they made decisions the way they did; their culture and the prosecutors in these cases encouraged them to do so. Considering the psychologically stressful nature of being asked to determine if a particular person should live or die (something for which no juror volunteered), it makes sense that the jurors would fall back and rely on comfortable cultural messages that provide a sense of order and normality—especially once the prosecutors encouraged them to. Simply put, it might just be asking too much of jurors to juggle the stress of determining whether someone lives or dies and the stress of re-evaluating and challenging the cultural messages with which they have become accustomed.

Whatever its true cause, the conclusion that jurors either ignore, reject, or react with hostility toward contextualizing life history evidence is quite troubling. This conclusion indicates that it might not be possible to eliminate arbitrariness from the death sentencing process because jurors are discouraged (either by their culture or by prosecutors) from taking into account the tremendous differences that exist among capital defendants and particularly between capital defendants and their judgers. The use of individualizing discourses that deny the causal relevance of contextualizing evidence invariably causes racial inequality to be swept under the rug because it ignores the persistent and insidious effects of institutionalized, structural discrimination. Ironically, by ignoring racial inequality, the death penalty is able to remain a racist institution. Because black and Hispanic capital defendants are more likely to be drawn from areas conducive to lethal violence and are more likely to experience structural mitigation—things like concentrated disadvantage, violent neighborhoods, lack of social and cultural capital, and lack of educational and employment opportunities (Haney, 2004), denying the relevance of external social forces will inevitably disadvantage these groups and help to ensure the continued unequal application of the death penalty. If jurors are unable or unwilling to consider such evidence, then "the sentencing process is fatally flawed" (*Abdul-Kabir v. Quarterman*, 2007, p. 264) because they will be incapable of engaging in the "reasoned moral response" (*California v. Brown*, 1987, p. 545) required by the Constitution.

Chapter 5
"A Premeditated Intent to Kill": Hegemonic Tales in Judicial Sentencing Opinions

> "These murders do not reflect a hair trigger on a gun discharging during a robbery. They reflect, instead, a premeditated intent to kill. There is nothing to show accident, negligence, recklessness or anything short of a deliberate and planned murder of two people."

> "This is not a case of a robbery gone bad, nor a 'drive by' random shooting. The original intention was and remained to do one thing and that was to kill [victim]."

> "… the reasonable doubt shared by the Court and jury that [defendant] fired the fatal shot is a mitigating circumstance which cannot be outweighed by any array of circumstances presented here"

The analysis now turns to the decision making expressed by judges in their written sentencing opinions. The decision making of judges in capital trials has never been analyzed, but considering their role as judicial elites, judges have an extraordinary power to frame cultural narratives. The extensive legal training of judges—along with the structural protections afforded judges in Delaware (merit selection, 12-year terms)—suggests they may be more receptive to mitigating evidence than jurors, but prior research by Givelber and Farrell (2012) hints that judges are less receptive to defense evidence than jurors. So, the behavior of judges in capital cases is really an open question.

Given the dictates of the Supreme Court to consider *all* mitigating factors, one might expect that regardless of how they actually made their decisions, judges would at least give a balanced accounting of all penalty phase evidence followed by a conclusion that explains why the judge decided the aggravating evidence outweighed the mitigating evidence or *vice versa*. Yet, that is not what appears in these eight sentencing opinions. The analysis reveals a judiciary that—like jurors—is almost completely focused on the guilt-related question of culpability. Rather than weighing the evidence in aggravation against the evidence in mitigation, the judges seemed to default to individual responsibility in making their sentencing decisions. The crux of the judge's decision in seven of these eight cases was on whether or not he believed the defendant intended to cause the death for which he was convicted. Little, if any, attention was given to the evidence of the defendants' upbringings. Many opinions did not mention this evidence at all, and those that did made it clear that such evidence was not given much, if any, weight. In fact, one opinion even converted the structural mitigation into an aggravating circumstance! Like the jurors, if the judge was unsure of the defendant's role or intent in the crime, he imposed a life sentence, but if he had no doubt that the defendant intended his victim to die, he imposed a death sentence. Interestingly, this finding is even more pronounced in the life cases than it is in the death cases.

Sparing the Least Responsible

Considering the closely tied nature of individualism and vigilantism in American culture (Scheingold, 1984), the ways in which individualism fuels and justifies the death penalty (Dunn and Kaplan, 2009), and the fact that the defense is typically the only side to present any evidence challenging individualistic understandings of human behavior, one might expect to find more subversive stories told by judges who imposed a life sentence, but the data reveal the opposite conclusion! The opinions from the three life cases in which contextualizing mitigation was presented were *more* bound to individualistic constructions of human responsibility and did *less* to challenge hegemonic individualism. In fact, two of these three opinions made *no reference* to the defendant's life history whatsoever, and the third condensed the life history evidence into three sentences. Instead of discussing the impact of environmental factors on the defendants' behaviors, two of these opinions focused almost entirely on the defendants' intent and the third deferred entirely to the jury.

Donald: "Subject to Doubt"

Despite the use of two social workers to attempt to contextualize Donald's behavior by discussing his childhood experiences that pressured him to crime—being raised in a high crime neighborhood by his grandmother, his mother being involved in drugs, early exposure to violence in the home, and early involvement with antisocial peers—the sentencing judge did not make a single reference to Donald's social history in his sentencing opinion. In fact, his three-page sentencing opinion makes no reference to any sentencing phase evidence at all. Instead, he concurred with the seven jurors who recommended a life sentence because he was unable to determine who fired the fatal bullet:

> The Court ... shares the jury's reasonable doubt that [Donald] was the actual trigger-man and under the circumstances of this case cannot justify the imposition of a death sentence. There is no evidence that killing the clerk was part of the plan of robbery and it is clear from the surveillance tape that the shooting was impulsive even though intentional. In the Court's view only the actual shooter would possess the state of mind that would warrant imposition of the death penalty and the identity of that person is subject to doubt in this case.

> To put it in statutory terms, the reasonable doubt shared by the Court and jury that [Donald] fired the fatal shot is a mitigating circumstance which cannot be outweighed by any array of aggravating circumstances presented here.

Of course, a defendant's level of culpability is an important question, and the wording of the final sentence suggests that determining culpability may just be the first step in the judge's decision-making process. Maybe if the judge had determined that Donald's level of intent was sufficient for a death sentence, he would have then engaged in an analysis of the penalty phase evidence, including the contextualizing mitigation, to determine if Donald should be sentenced to death. However, by ignoring Donald's social history and focusing solely on culpability, the judge gave primacy to individualistic micro-level explanations for criminal behavior and thereby helped to reinforce and validate hegemonic individualism.

Roger: "The Court Agrees With the Jury"

Roger's trial provided one of the best opportunities for judges to contextualize criminal behavior because the mitigating life history evidence presented in his trial was more extensive and detailed than it was in most of the other cases and because his role as the shooter was not really in doubt (despite the efforts of defense counsel to implicate two of Roger's friends). Roger presented two social workers to describe his childhood in one of America's most violent, drug-infested cities, but the judge did not take the opportunity to place Roger's behavior into its larger social context. On the contrary, the sentencing opinion was less than two pages long and did not discuss any of the evidence presented in the trial. Despite the jury's seven-to-five vote in favor of life, the entire reasoning presented by the judge in the sentencing opinion was, "The Court agrees with the jury that the mitigating evidence clearly and substantially outweighs the aggravating evidence that has been presented and that a life sentence is therefore appropriate under the law." Nowhere does he state what the evidence was or why it was so convincing (especially considering the closeness of the jury's vote). This opinion, therefore, does not really support an individualistic worldview, but neither does it subvert hegemonic individualism. Considering the individualizing nature of the trial process itself (Haney, 2005), this opinion really leaves hegemonic individualism undisturbed.

Ted: "Committed With Criminal Negligence"

Ted's mitigation case was also extremely detailed. Along with Roger, Ted presented the greatest number of mitigating circumstances derived from his life history. Through a psychologist and a forensic nurse, Ted presented evidence that he was an unwanted child who witnessed and experienced extreme neglect and abuse and was basically forced to begin living on the street by the time he was 11 years old. Of the three life cases in which life history evidence was presented, Ted's is the only one where the judge even mentioned such evidence, but he relegated the extensive evidence of Ted's childhood experiences of victimization to three sentences out of an 11-page opinion:

> Defendant was an "unwanted" child who grew up in a neglectful and unsafe home, with a father who in effect lived two lives—one with his family and the other with his "girlfriends." Defendant's father made no attempt to rectify or disguise this facet of his relationship with his family. In contrast to his other siblings, all of whom were older, Defendant had no real relationship with his father, as evidenced by the fact that one time, Defendant's father abandoned him on the porch of the house he was living in while separated from Defendant's mother.

This summary hardly does justice to the horrors and the emotional pain described in Chapter 3 that Ted experienced as a child, the difficulties he had, or the influence these events had on his development. While it would be unreasonable to expect a sentencing opinion to capture the full extent of any defendant's physical and emotional traumas, this opinion substantially condensed considerable mitigating circumstances and included no discussion of the likely influence they had on Ted's criminal choices. In fact, nowhere in the conclusion does the judge make any further reference to Ted's childhood. Instead he focused on the nature of the crime and Ted's intent, agreeing with the nine jurors who voted for life because "at most the jury has found that the Defendant acted with a criminally negligent state of mind."

So, again, although the end result was a life sentence, this sentencing opinion helps construct the hegemonic story of individual responsibility. The evidence offered an excellent opportunity to subvert taken-for-granted views of criminal behavior, but the judge passed on that opportunity and based his sentence entirely on the guilt-stage question of intent. The fact that Ted was likely significantly impacted by factors beyond his control is completely ignored, and the entire focus of the inquiry is on his level of culpability. Therefore, the judge reinforces the idea that one's intent is all that matters, no matter what factors may have impacted the decision making of the perpetrator. None of this is meant to suggest that Ted did not make choices or that he does not deserve to be punished for his role in the killing of another human being. However, capital mitigation is supposed to help decision makers understand how and why people come to the decisions they do and to reduce the penalty for those whose decisions to kill may have been influenced by traumas over which they had no control. By ignoring such influences, these three sentencing opinions help to support an incomplete view of human behavior that views humans as the sole causal agents and ignores the powerful effects of social structural forces.

Death to the Most Responsible

The findings reviewed above suggest that hegemonic discourses are so powerful that they even infect life decisions, but, as mentioned during the discussion of the sentencing opinion in Donald's case, it is possible that judicial sentencing decisions are made in a two-step process: the first step to determine if the defendant is culpable enough to be put to death and a second step that then weighs aggravating evidence against mitigating evidence. The four death opinions, however, suggest that there is no second step. Although jurists in the death cases did mention the life history evidence in their opinions, none of the death opinions truly explored this evidence or appeared to give it any weight. Rather, it seems as if the judges included such evidence to ensure their opinions—which would be automatically reviewed by the Delaware Supreme Court—passed appellate review. The wording of the opinions suggested that such contextualizing evidence had little bearing on the sentencing decisions of the judges and that they based their sentencing decisions on the defendants' level of intent or premeditation.

Steve: "Dysfunctional Background is Now Set and Immutable"

Steve's trial represents one of the most troubling uses of mitigating life history evidence. As described in Chapter 3, Steve's father abandoned him at age three, and Steve experienced a "chaotic childhood" in which he received no love, support, or validation until his mother began dating the man who eventually convinced him to participate in three murders, including the two for which he was convicted in this trial. This older man treated Steve like his own son and gave him the love he had been craving his entire life. Yet, the judge transformed these mitigating factors into aggravating ones! Rather than using Steve's upbringing as a way of explaining Steve's behavior or considering it as a reason he might not deserve death (*California v. Brown*, 1987), he used them to predict Steve's future dangerousness and then concluded that regardless of any impact these factors may have had, Steve still made a choice.

Unlike the sentencing opinions in the life cases that either did not mention the life history evidence or barely grazed the surface, the judge in Steve's trial spent nearly five pages detailing Steve's background and the influence the co-perpetrator had over his behavior. He mentioned that Steve has numerous relatives involved with crime, that his biological father disappeared when he was three, and that his life was full of risk factors. He even conceded that Steve "came from a significantly dysfunctional family background which had virtually no moral compass and left him vulnerable to a negative father figure like [co-defendant]." He went on to admit, "His family history explains what he is. [The co-defendant] became his father figure." However, rather than using this conclusion as a mitigating circumstance, the judge argued, "All of [Steve's] risk factors and predictors are historical in nature. That is they are set and cannot be changed. Those, therefore, predicting his behavior, as evidenced by three murders, remain," and in his conclusion, the judge reiterated this point: "[Steve's] dysfunctional background is now set and immutable. It has manifested itself in three murders."

While the above excerpts suggest a sort of retributive determinism that, in a way, challenges hegemonic individualism, the opinion needs to be conveyed in its entirety and placed in its own context. These killings garnered a lot of media attention because of the youth and supposed innocence of the victims, so it seems likely that the judge was especially careful to include all the details of the penalty phase. Furthermore, despite acknowledging the possible influence of environmental influences, the judge fails to acknowledge that changing the environment could still have an impact on Steve's behavior. It seems as if his character was entirely created by his childhood and "cannot be changed." This actually serves to de-contextualize behavior because it makes it seem like the inevitable product of things that came before rather than the result of a decision that is influenced by both past experiences and present evaluations of possible modes of conduct. Present circumstances can also mold one's view of perceived options, so to truly contextualize behavior, one needs to acknowledge that changing the context would likely have a profound effect on behavior.

In addition, when the opinion is read in its entirety, the judge's focus on individual culpability becomes apparent. He still treats Steve's decision to engage in these murders as the result of a purely unburdened free will, views Steve's actions as illustrative of his character, and bases his death decision on the apparent premeditation involved. The fact that Steve clearly intended the deaths of the victims was the primary consideration:

> To say these shootings were anything less than a cold-blooded execution would be an injustice. These murders do not reflect a hair trigger on a gun discharging during a robbery. They reflect, instead, a premeditated intention to kill. There is nothing to show accident, negligence, recklessness or anything short of a deliberate and planned murder of two people.

As the judge put it, mitigating factors "go only so far" and since Steve made a "choice to participate" in a "plan … to kill," the mitigators do not really matter. Therefore, the judge rejects the mitigating impact of contextualizing evidence and actually re-affirms the dominant cultural narrative despite acknowledging Steve's background and its powerful influence. In rejecting the relevance of the co-perpetrator's influence, the judge stated:

> … [T]here was a year between the [prior] murder [by the defendant and co-defendant] and the murder of [the victims in this case]. This is more than adequate time to have reflected on his choice of committing the ultimate crime in [year of first murder] before doing it again. He chose to help [co-defendant] in [year of first murder], he has said, because of his love for him and not wanting to disappoint him. That explanation may work once. It disappears after a year.

Rather than realizing how the power of love may have compelled Steve to act in ways he may not have otherwise acted, since Steve "chose" not to repudiate the only fatherly love he had ever received, the judge decided Steve was *more* deserving of a death sentence! In other words, even though people crave acceptance and will therefore attempt to emulate the behavior of those they admire and will do almost anything to gain the approval of those they love, the love Steve received from the co-perpetrator after being involved in the first killing should have somehow diminished rather than increased his likelihood of being involved in another killing. Overall, the opinion treats Steve's choice to kill as a rational calculation of all possible modes of conduct rather than a decision made in a context that involved coercion, emotion, fear, and perceived barriers to action and included a confluence of factors that are unlikely to interact in the same way again (at least not in prison).

This is not to say that the judge was wrong in determining that the aggravating factors in Steve's trial outweighed the mitigating ones, nor is it to suggest that he was wrong to conclude that mitigating factors can "go only so far." Capital sentencing in Delaware is supposed to involve a subjective determination of how much relative weight to give aggravating and mitigating circumstances, and as long as he considers all the evidence, the judge is well within his rights to say that the mitigating circumstances pale in comparison to the aggravating ones. The key finding about this sentencing opinion is that despite acknowledging the subversive story that prior experiences may have an influence on behavior, the judge transformed the mitigators into aggravators, focused on Steve's choice to kill, suggested that Steve was incapable of changing (and was therefore inherently evil), and thereby still relied upon and reinforced hegemonic narratives of individual responsibility and dispositional attribution in his sentencing opinion.

Charlie: "Monstrous Murderous Actions"

As in Steve's case, the judge discussed the presented life history evidence in the sentencing opinion of Charlie's trial, but the overall theme presented in the sentencing opinion was one of individual responsibility. The judge wrote that he was "uneasy about" the contextualizing mitigation Charlie presented and he discounted the defense experts' testimonies because Charlie's mother was "acting out of her own perception of what was best for her son" and she did not "physically abuse her son," as if this somehow diminished the impact of her decisions to pull Charlie from special education or to avoid much needed counseling. The judge also countered his discussion of the defendant's childhood by pointing out that Charlie did not come "from a dysfunctional family," nor did he live in poverty or "a high crime neighborhood." Furthermore, in his conclusion, the judge pointed out that the defendant had "no psychosis of any kind," suggesting that his lack of counseling or parental involvement were less important since they were not factors within the defendant. Overall, the sentencing opinion downplayed the importance of childhood development on one's personality and instead focused its attention on individual factors, showing the importance of commonsense understandings of behavior on the decisions of professionally trained judges and the way judicial sentencing opinions help to construct commonsense cultural narratives.

In clear contrast to his dismissal of Charlie's life history, the judge gave significant credence to Charlie's criminal history, concluding, "There is a clear propensity for violence, especially violence involving guns," as if his actions were a manifestation of the type of person Charlie is rather than the circumstances in which he found himself. Regarding the murder itself, the judge determined, "This was no casual, impromptu, drive-by shooting. [Defendant] knew [victim] or knew who he was. The conversation between [defendant] and [a witness] … reveals a strong undercurrent of premeditation." This language suggests that Charlie is an evil person who inherently chooses to solve problems with violence rather than a person living within a social context that promotes violent solutions to problems or a person who only felt acceptance by people who taught him to value crime and violence (Anderson, 1999; Cohen, 1955; Sutherland, 1947; Wolfgang and Ferracuti, 1967). Rather than discuss how the defendant came to his choices because of his inability to succeed at other endeavors, the lack of help he received for his problems, the sense of rejection he felt, or the social norms that existed in his subculture, the judge detailed the circumstances of the crime absent any social context. He mentioned that Charlie "was careful to disguise himself," stressed that the "killing was planned," and described the murder as "nothing short of a cold blooded execution" in which Charlie "relentlessly continued to shoot at" the victim, even standing over him after he was down and "shot him in the head." In agreeing with the jury's unanimous recommendation for a death sentence, the judge focused his sentencing opinion on "the particular circumstances and details of the commission of these killings," dehumanized Charlie and his behavior—as if the killings were the work of an anonymous monster rather than of a human being who experienced a social environment that greatly impacted his development—by referring to his conduct as "monstrous murderous actions," and concluded that Charlie's intent and planning was the aggravating factor that "weighs most heavily" in his decision.

Michael: "Like Jackals Lurking at a Water Hole"

While Michael's attorneys did attempt to contextualize his behavior, they utilized no expert testimony and relied solely on the second-hand stories of Michael's relatives. Therefore, the judge was not given much of an opportunity to contextualize Michael's behavior. Nevertheless, the judge spent most of the paragraph in which he mentioned Michael's life history trying to minimize its importance, eventually concluding that "the Court cannot conclude that [Michael]'s upbringing was so bad as to constitute a mitigating circumstance" because "his father did not abandon him" and "his father provided support and exercised his right to visitation," as if that makes his father's absence or the abuse the defendant suffered during his teen years any less traumatic or influential on his development. It may not be Michael's father's fault that he had no knowledge of Michael's whereabouts, but Michael was still deprived of his father. The judge could have discussed the likely effects of this reality or the potential impact of being abused during his critical teenage years, but instead he dismissed the impact of these experiences because Michael's father did not deliberately inflict these traumas on Michael. This, too, supports an individualistic worldview—only intentionally caused harms matter.

In justifying a death sentence in which five jurors opposed a death penalty, the judge referred to the crime as "a ruthless act of human predation," described Michael and the co-perpetrator as "jackals lurking at a water hole," and explained that Michael's actions were his overriding concern: "The circumstances of the crime and criminality of the defendants are aggravating circumstances of overwhelming weight." The use of the adjective "overwhelming" gives the impression that very few (if any) pieces of evidence could have overcome the actions of the defendants. The judge seems to have implied that even if he had presented a detailed life history defense, it would not have mattered because the factors that may or may not have constrained his available options could not possibly outweigh the actions themselves. Again, this is not to suggest that the judge made the wrong decision in this case or that the "circumstances of the crime and criminality of the defendants" do not deserve great weight in determining a sentence, but this one sentence suggests that the actions of killers during their crimes are the *only things* that are relevant, as if a human being can be understood by the worst thing he ever did or that his behavior is a reflection of his true character and not a symptom of the experiences he has accumulated over a lifetime.

Jerry: "The True Character of the Defendant as Revealed by His Crime"

As explained in Chapter 3, Jerry did not offer any contextualizing evidence. The bulk of the mitigation case focused on arguing that neither alleged statutory aggravator was proven to exist beyond a reasonable doubt. Nevertheless, the entire tone of the sentencing opinion suggested that the only thing the judge needed to know was what Jerry had done at the time of the crime. In his words, the mitigating circumstances "are insubstantial when compared to the nature of the crime and *the true character of the defendant as revealed by his crime and by his conduct*" (emphasis added). Again, it is perfectly reasonable for the judge to conclude that the aggravating factors substantially outweigh the mitigating ones, but the suggestion that one's true character can be revealed by a single action (no matter how horrific) at a single point in time without any reference to the external, contextual factors that may have influenced those decisions implies that the judge would not have been swayed by any array of mitigating circumstances. Overall, the text of the ten-page opinion focused on Jerry's decisions and his criminal history. He treated Jerry's decisions as rational calculations unencumbered by social environment. For example, even though there were no witnesses to the killing and the evidence was equivocal as to whether Jerry's planning and cover-up began before or after he killed his wife, the judge opined:

> All of the planning ... was being done by [Jerry]. It included *careful planning* for the murder of [the victim] after the effective date of the new insurance policy

> on her life. His plan was to lure her to meet him … where he would kill her with his .357 magnum revolver by shooting her in the head. His intent was to leave her body for discovery in her parked car … He hoped that the murder would be unsolved and he developed a scheme to mislead the police so it would go unsolved. (emphasis added)

Later, he wrote:

> Here, there were several opportunities for [Jerry] to abandon his plan of murder but at every stage *he chose* death for [the victim]. *He chose* death for [the victim] so he could collect insurance on her life. *He chose* death for [the victim] as part of his plan to live with a mistress. (emphasis added)

Despite the evidence presented of the positive things Jerry had done and the positive impact he had on his family and friends, the overriding theme throughout the sentencing opinion was that Jerry is simply a bad person.

Alan's Trial: A Subversive Story

Although the first seven sentencing opinions reviewed all utilized hegemonic tales that help to reinforce individualistic understandings of human behavior, there was one sentencing opinion that utilized a subversive story. Ironically, it was in Alan's trial, the only one in which *no evidence* from the defendant's past was presented at all. Even Jerry presented evidence that his brother was born with severe mental and physical handicaps and that his parents also raised about 30 foster children, many of whom had psychological problems. Jerry's defense did not contextualize any of this information or explain how it could be connected to his murder, but the defense attorneys in Alan's trial did not mention a single fact of Alan's upbringing. Interestingly, the jurors who voted for life in Alan's trial were the only jurors in the entire sample who did not base their recommendation on the defendant's culpability, and the judge in Alan's case also appeared to avoid using doubts as to Alan's culpability (and there were significant doubts) as his sentencing rationale and instead contextualized Alan's behavior.

Even though no evidence could determine whether Alan or a co-perpetrator fired the fatal bullet, the prosecution's key witness had credibility issues, the jury was hung in Alan's first trial, and the jury in the re-trial deliberated guilt for three days, the judge did not focus on these doubts in his sentencing opinion. Instead, he gave a balanced accounting of Alan's level of responsibility, his youth and immaturity, the circumstances of the crime, and the impact his execution would have on his family. Despite the lack of any mitigating life history evidence, the sentencing opinion attempted to place Alan's actions within a social context and to humanize Alan by talking about his family and children and the effect he has on them, the fact that Alan was a well-behaved inmate, and Alan's immaturity.

He even noted the finding of the psychologist who "concluded that Defendant is not a danger to himself, nor to other inmates, *given his environment* [in prison]" (emphasis added), suggesting context matters. The judge did mention Alan's level of culpability, but he did not make it his primary consideration:

> The evidence supports the conclusion that both Defendants participated in the attempted robbery, both fired a handgun during the attempted robbery, and no particular individual was the leader or mastermind of the event. In fact, the evidence would suggest that the idea of robbing the [victim] was hatched on the same evening it occurred without a great deal of organization or thought as to how it would occur or the possible ramifications if things went wrong. *This was simply a crime of opportunity performed by two immature individuals who at that moment exhibited a thug mentality* … (emphasis added)

While this excerpt did utilize the defendants' lack of planning and equal culpability to help the judge reach a decision in a similar vein as the other life cases described above, it did something different as well. It noted the importance of context and the immaturity of the defendants. Rather than suggesting that the crime represents the true underlying characters of the defendants, the judge in this case suggested they were "immature" and that the crime was one "of opportunity." The clear implication is that given a different confluence of events and a chance to mature, the actions of these defendants may very well have been different. In his conclusion the judge used human fallibility to again emphasize why these defendants should not get the ultimate punishment: "As outrageous and senseless as this killing may have been, the *history and background* of these defendant[s] does not reflect a situation where death is the only appropriate consequence. They have committed *a horrible mistake* that they will now pay for the rest of their lives" (emphasis added). Like the judges in the other life cases, this judge could have easily stated that doubts as to Alan's intent or the origin of the fatal bullet led him to conclude that Alan did not deserve to die. He did not do this. He took steps to place Alan's actions within a social milieu and show that his actions were not completely the product of an unburdened free will. He suggested Alan's behavior was the result of his youth and immaturity, thus the opinion directly challenged the basic tenets of hegemonic individualism and wove a subversive story.

Conclusion

These eight sentencing opinions are quite revealing as to the operation of mitigation and the power of hegemonic discourses. The overall focus in seven of these opinions was on individual responsibility and culpability; only one opinion offered a subversive tale. This reveals that even among professionally trained, highly experienced judges who are insulated from the whims of public opinion, there is a predominant preoccupation with models of criminal behavior that focus on micro-level questions of free will and internal problems. This reveals both the power of hegemonic tales and the ways in which capital cases are able to reinforce and reaffirm individualistic mentalities. Culpability and crime heinousness are certainly relevant factors in capital sentencing decisions and judges would be expected to detail these facts, but seven of these opinions make it seem like these were the *only* factors the judges considered and constructed the idea that individual responsibility is the only real concern. This flies in the face of the Supreme Court's jurisprudence on mitigation and it helps to support hegemonic individualism.

As with the findings on juror behavior, these conclusions are not meant as a criticism of judges or their eventual conclusions. Judges are forced to utilize the evidence presented to them when making a decision. They cannot do their own investigation or draw conclusions unsupported by the evidence. Secondly, judges have the power to determine how much weight to give each piece of evidence, and they make this determination based upon the issues they find most compelling and relevant. Therefore, what this analysis suggests is the power of hegemonic individualism. Much like the defendants before them who made decisions to commit violent acts within a social and cultural context that condones or even promotes violence and aggression, sentencing decisions are made within a social, cultural, and institutional setting that promotes individualistic ways of viewing the world, and judges are strongly impacted by these commonsense views of the world. Judges' decisions, like those of jurors, are necessarily and inherently influenced by the deep-rooted nature of individualism in American culture and its legal system. However, as judicial elites, they also help to validate the core tenets of individualism, a fact that exposes the true power of hegemonic tales: they are often self-perpetuating. By influencing the claims-makers, hegemonic narratives are able to reinforce themselves.

As with the finding that jurors are preoccupied with culpability, this finding indicates that it may not be possible to craft capital sentencing statutes that do not result in arbitrary decisions. In *none* of these opinions was there any attempt to address racial or structural inequality. In fact, the opinions do not even mention the races of either the victims or the defendants. As with the presentation of mitigation by attorneys and in the interviews with jurors, racial inequality was completely swept under the rug. Therefore, the findings of this chapter combined with Givelber and Farrell's (2012) finding that judges are *less* receptive to defense evidence and *more* racist in their non-capital verdict decisions than jurors are and statistical analyses that suggest that Delaware currently experiences race-based sentencing disparities that are "substantially more pronounced than in other jurisdictions" (Johnson et al., 2012, p. 1954) suggest that despite the claims of the Delaware General Assembly that judges would be less arbitrary than juries,[1] entrusting professionally trained judges with the final sentencing authority is unlikely to

1 Fleury-Steiner, et al. (2009) detail how the legislators who argued in favor of the 1991 law change that put final sentencing authority in the hands of judges argued that judges would be less arbitrary than juries.

make the death sentencing process any less arbitrary. Part of the reason for this could be that using individualistic rationales helps to bolster the color-blindness that obscures the enduring racial divide in opportunities (Bonilla-Silva, 2010; Brown et al., 2003; Oliver and Shapiro, 1995). When important background factors are trivialized, differently situated defendants may be judged similarly because important differentiating evidence from their life histories may be getting either cursory treatment or ignored altogether. When people from different circumstances are treated "equally," they are impacted differently, but this reality is "whitewashed" (Brown et al., 2003) by commonsense individualism. Since minority defendants are more likely to experience social forces conducive to lethal violence—what Haney (2004) calls "structural mitigation"—than whites are, ignoring or downplaying the important role environmental factors play in human decision making likely disadvantages poor and minority defendants and increases their odds of a death sentence. This type of reasoning not only appears to contradict the dictates of the Supreme Court's more recent mitigation rulings, but it also leaves the contemporary death penalty little different from the scheme rejected by the Court in *Furman v. Georgia* (1972).

Conclusion
Individualism, Public Policy, and the Future of Capital Punishment

This in-depth, qualitative examination of the mitigation process in Delaware is the first to examine the life of mitigating evidence from its presentation through final sentencing decision, and as such, it is quite informative as to the effect cultural messages and images can have in affecting juridical outcomes and the challenges of crafting capital sentencing statutes that are able to avoid the arbitrariness that has traditionally plagued the sentence of death. Cultural patterns are important for understanding the means and intensity of punishment a society deems appropriate because they "structure the ways in which we think about criminals, providing the intellectual frameworks ... through which we see these individuals, understand their motivations, and dispose of them as cases" (Garland, 1990, p. 195). This study is able to demonstrate the real world life and death consequences of this reality. Taking advantage of a unique capital sentencing statute in Delaware, this study was able to document the ways in which mitigating evidence is presented by defense attorneys and experts and the ways in which both jurors and judges respond to this evidence. In this way, it was able to examine the ways in which micro-level, individualistic understandings of human behavior do or do not influence the mitigation process. In the process, it illustrated the shortcomings of the law in being able to overcome internalized, commonsensical understandings of human behavior and the ways in which mitigation is and is not able to challenge these taken-for-granted assumptions.

This study traced the presentation of mitigating evidence in eight capital trials (four life and four death cases) and has shown that the mitigation cases presented by capital defense attorneys often simultaneously tell both hegemonic tales of individual responsibility *and* subversive stories of social causation. In Dunn and Kaplan's (2009) study, they concluded that the presentation of life history evidence tended to reinforce individualism because the presentation of such evidence placed the onus of the problems discussed entirely within the defendant. These eight mitigation cases reveal a much different pattern. In all eight trials, defense attorneys argued that the defendant should be spared because he was not culpable enough to warrant a death sentence and because LWOP was retributive and incapacitating enough. However, in five trials the defense team also presented expert testimony that challenged the dominant cultural narrative that individuals are the sole causal agents. This evidence included a discussion of how risk factors that were outside of the defendant and beyond his control increased his risk for being involved in crime and even attempted to explain why some who experiences a given risk factor are able to avoid criminality. In a sixth trial, the defense attempted to present some contextualizing evidence from the defendant's past, but they used no experts and did not make an explicit connection between the defendant's past experiences of victimization and his subsequent violent behavior. In addition, all of the attorneys presented evidence that attempted to humanize their clients and show them as embedded in a web of social and familial relationships—to depict them not as monsters but as people who are capable of both good and bad.

These attempts at subverting the dominant cultural story by offering contextualizing data were met with extreme resistance, even by jurors who voted for a life sentence. Dunn and Kaplan asked, "Are there tools outside the psy-complex that could be used to avoid death sentences while simultaneously combating destructive individualism? Or is our legal system so fundamentally individualizing that it is incapable of hearing other accounts of the human experience" (2009, p. 363)? Based upon the answers given by these 35 jurors and the judicial sentencing opinions in these eight cases, it appears that the system may be deaf to other accounts, making it difficult to win a sentence of less than death while also challenging the culture of individualism. None of the jurors relied upon the defendant's life history when making their sentencing recommendations. In light of the findings by Sundby (1997) that jurors tend to view defense experts negatively, it is not surprising that jurors rejected the life history evidence presented by these experts, but the results of this study help to offer a theoretical explanation for why that is: jurors are beholden to an individualistic discourse that rejects the causal theories of these so-called "experts" unless lay experts are able to bring the "power and truth of personal observation" (Sundby, 1997, p. 1145) to support them. As revealed by the interviews, most of the jurors in this sample could not recall the contextualizing life history evidence even when given explicit reminders, and perhaps more significantly, those who did recall it either dismissed it as irrelevant or were downright hostile to it. The interviews reveal that the primary reason given by jurors for opposing a death sentence was doubt as to culpability and the primary rationale for supporting a death sentence was being convinced that the defendant intended the victim's death. Only three jurors gave a different account—all three based their life recommendations on the defense's ability to humanize the defendant and show the effects his execution would have on his family members.

Even though judges are strategically placed to provide data on the functioning of mitigation, the decision making of trial judges in capital cases had never been analyzed prior to this study. As judicial elites, their opinions help to construct cultural master narratives, but as highly experienced, trained, and educated jurists, they should have a better understanding of the relevance of mitigating evidence and be better positioned to utilize such evidence. This is especially true in Delaware, where judges are appointed to 12-year terms through a merit selection process that helps to insulate them from the pressure of public opinion. Yet, the data collected here suggest that, for the most part, judges are also greatly influenced by hegemonic individualism and do little to question its basic tenets.

That is, even among judges, the law has a very limited ability to overcome taken-for-granted cultural assumptions. Seven of the eight opinions suggest that judges based their sentencing decisions almost entirely on culpability. Three of the life opinions either did not mention contextualizing evidence or dealt with it in an extremely cursory way. The four death opinions tried to minimize the weight or relevance of mitigating circumstances; one even converted the mitigating evidence into aggravating evidence. Only one of the eight opinions offered a subversive story that called into question the basic assumptions of hegemonic individualism, and this occurred in a case in which no life history evidence was even presented! As with the jurors' recommendations, the opinions suggest that judges imposed a life sentence if they had doubts as to the defendant's culpability and imposed a death sentence if they did not harbor such doubts. Contextualizing life history evidence did not factor into these decisions.

The Importance of These Findings

While these findings may be interesting, it is not immediately clear why they are important. After all, the entire point of the jury system is to have jurors act as the conscience of the community and apply community standards to criminal cases. However, the conclusion that decision makers in capital cases are overly reliant on psychological individualism exposes a stark reality that calls into question the ability of guided discretion statutes to limit the death penalty's arbitrariness and the ability of social policy in the United States more generally to address the true causes of social problems such as crime, poverty, and entrenched inequality. This is not to suggest that individualistic, micro-level theories of human action are wrong. Humans certainly make decisions, are able to exercise free will, and can be deterred by the threat of legal sanctions. However, such explanations are overly simplistic and incomplete. They do not capture the full range of factors that impact human behavior or even the factors that influence our decisions. Although people make choices, those choices are enabled and constrained by forces beyond their control. As Dunn and Kaplan put it, "Humans are agents, but they act within particular socio-historical contexts that limit perceived and material possibilities for action" (2009, p. 364). In other words, "The causes of criminal conduct are multifaceted" (Pratt et al., 2008, p. 383).

To argue that someone who was abused *in utero* and then left to fend for himself by the time he was a teenager had the same opportunities and ability to make the same choices as anyone else is either to remain deliberately ignorant of or to discount the importance of social structural conditions on human decision making. It is, in essence, a manner of denying someone of the very feature that makes him or her human—the fact that his or her behavior is social in nature. For many violent young men, violence is viewed as necessary—not as a choice. To them, violence is a survival strategy that is used to avoid being victimized (Anderson, 1999; Mansley, 2009), so an overreliance on an individualistic/free will perspective ends up either missing or masking the important role of social context, racial and structural inequality, and formative life experiences in affecting human decisions and behavior. Acknowledging that human beings are social creatures who are strongly impacted by their social environments does not absolve them of responsibility for their actions, nor does it suggest that criminals should be treated leniently. However, the hegemony of individualism does absolve society of responsibility for the great harms it has inflicted on its members and its role in creating conditions conducive to lethal violence while simultaneously disempowering the rest of society from devising meaningful social solutions to social problems such as crime and poverty. Therefore, capital sentencing decisions need to take into account *both* individualistic factors such as culpability *and* contextualizing factors like exposure to violent neighborhoods, and American individualism acts as a cultural force that impedes complete and lucid understandings of criminal behavior, not to mention a whole host of other social issues.

Implications for the Death Penalty

Most directly, the findings in this book call into question the ability of human actors to apply the ultimate sentence in a manner that does not offend the Constitution. The Supreme Court has repeatedly ruled that the reliability of death sentences is premised on a full and complete consideration of mitigating circumstances and that evidence derived from a defendant's background is *central* to such considerations (*California v. Brown*, 1987; *Eddings v. Oklahoma*, 1982; *Penry v. Lynaugh*, 1989; *Rompilla v. Beard*, 2005; *Tennard v. Dretke*, 2004; *Wiggins v. Smith*, 2003; *Williams v. Taylor*, 2000; *Woodson v. North Carolina*, 1976). Yet, the results reported here suggest that such considerations are not taking place. In fact, the results of this study suggest that sentencing decisions are being based almost entirely on guilt-stage evidence, which challenges the entire logic of the bifurcated capital trial, which was supposed to reduce arbitrariness. Rather than guiding the discretion of capital jurors (and judges), bifurcated capital trials may simply be hampering the ability of defense attorneys to save their clients' lives. Instead of splitting the jury's decision into two parts, all the bifurcated trial seems to accomplish is preventing the defense from offering contextualizing evidence that may challenge the hegemonic discourse until *after* the jurors have made up their mind. Considering many (or most) mitigating factors will be derived from a defendant's upbringing and life history (American Bar Association, 2003; American Bar Association, 2008; Haney, 2005), bifurcation may simply be preventing jurors from giving true consideration to mitigation.

This is not to suggest that capital jurors or judges *never* consider contextual mitigation. On the contrary, there are certainly examples of capital jurors who do consider such evidence, but as Sundby (1997) notes, this typically requires defense attorneys to orchestrate a balanced mitigation case that involves professional experts, lay experts, and family members of the defendant. Such orchestration, however, is extremely difficult, requires the existence of just the right evidence, and needs to be presented by a skillful defense team. Therefore, it happens incredibly rarely—rarely enough to be wanton and freakish. In this entire sample, Donald's case is the only one in which the type of orchestration envisioned by Sundby (1997) was even attempted. Interestingly, even in this case, the jurors were focused predominantly on culpability and ignored the contextual mitigation, basing their recommendations on whether or not they were convinced Donald was the actual trigger-man. Furthermore, the responses of several jurors in this study suggest that they may be mitigation impaired and therefore should have been excluded from service (*Morgan v. Illinois*, 1992). This study cannot determine whether better jury selection procedures could remedy the problems identified by these interviews, but prior legal precedent and empirical research suggests that eliminating such jurors from capital juries is extremely difficult, if not impossible (see Sandys and McClelland, 2003). Therefore, it seems unlikely that better jury selection is the answer.

If guided discretion statutes are only able to get decision makers in capital cases to give appropriate consideration to relevant evidence derived from defendants' upbringings in incredibly rare circumstances, then the death penalty is doomed to remain a racist institution. It has been repeatedly demonstrated the death penalty is not being applied in a race-neutral manner, and this phenomenon is not limited to the south. For example, Baldus, et al. (1998) found that death sentences in Philadelphia, PA, disadvantage black defendants, even when controlling for relevant case characteristics, and in just the last ten years, state-level studies have found racially discriminatory sentencing outcomes in capital cases in Texas (Urbina, 2003), California (Pierce and Radelet, 2005; Urbina, 2003), Missouri (Lenza et al., 2005), Maryland (Paternoster and Brame, 2008), Connecticut (Donohue, 2011), and Delaware (Johnson et al., 2012). The findings simply replicate the findings of studies conducted all across the United States since Baldus and his colleagues (1983) first published their findings of the effect of race on sentencing outcomes in Georgia in their failed effort to help Warren McCleskey avoid an execution.[1]

There are obviously other forces at work that help to maintain the racial *status quo* in capital sentencing outcomes, but hegemonic individualism likely also plays an important role in maintaining this discriminatory reality. If criminal sentences reflect cultural themes, then they will inevitably reflect the social inequality that is sustained by those cultural themes and will prevent any attempt at eliminating arbitrariness from capital sentencing from being effective. Because American culture values individualistic understandings of criminal conduct that explain crime as a freely chosen behavior (Scheingold, 1984; Scheingold, 1991), Americans have difficulty understanding the fact that choices are made within a social milieu that can either enhance or diminish possibilities for action or

1 For a comprehensive review of the older literature on the death penalty's racist application, see Baldus and Woodworth (2003).

accounting for the objective, observable social patterns to crime and criminality. Ignorance of these social patterns inherently harms those groups most afflicted by crime, violence, and factors conducive to crime and violence. The focus on individual responsibility makes it impossible to discuss issues of structural or racial inequality in any meaningful or sociologically informed manner. Because African Americans and other minorities are likely to experience mitigating contextual influences more acutely than white Americans are and capital defendants are disproportionately drawn from the ranks of the poor and people of color, the failure of capital sentencing decisions to give such factors true consideration adversely affects minority capital defendants more so than it does white ones (Haney, 2004). Therefore, structural and racial inequalities are quite often perpetuated and exacerbated by the law and by legal agents.

It is telling that none of the defense attorneys in these trials even attempted to address issues of racial inequality despite the fact that six of the defendants were non-whites. The color-blind logic of psychological individualism tells us that as long as there are no legal barriers to movement and opportunity, race no longer matters, but by remaining silent on the issue of entrenched racial inequality, it is much harder for the defense to educate jurors about the importance of a defendant's life history in order to get them to consider mitigating circumstances other than culpability. Entrenched, systematic, chronic, institutionalized racial discrimination is a fact of daily life for most African Americans, but through the ideology of individualism, where individuals are blamed for their own failings, the persistent pernicious effects of institutional discrimination can be ignored. Since most capital jurors are white, they have a difficult time empathizing with a defendant's plight, and this failure is partially the result of the fact that most jurors have not had any experiences that are remotely comparable to what the defendant has suffered (Haney, 2004). When combined with the fact that white capital jurors are especially unlikely to empathize with black defendants to begin with, individualistic worldviews make it nearly impossible for decision makers "to appreciate the role of social history and present circumstances in shaping the life course of African Americans. In capital cases, it interferes with the jurors' ability to take structural mitigation into account ..." (Haney, 2004, p. 1583). Therefore, in order for jurors to fully appreciate the relevance of life history evidence, they must also be educated about the role of racial inequality in society. When they are not, minority capital defendants are disadvantaged.

None of the defense teams in this sample, however, addressed such race-based issues, and as such, none of the judges (all of whom were white men) bothered to even mention the races of the defendants or victims or grappled with the effects of racial inequality. Only one juror even mentioned the idea of race, but this was done in a way that ignored racial inequality and focused on individualistic explanations for murder. Instead of addressing the ways in which social structures keep certain groups down, this juror said, "... they're hurting their own people because that's where the biggest problem is, with blacks killing blacks." He implied that the jurors had a new kind of white man's burden in that they had to send "a message and protecting even a certain race, protecting from themselves," as if their problems were brought on by themselves. As Fleury-Steiner put it, some jurors "tell stories of black-on-black violence that imply a taken-for-granted understanding of violence as something to which blacks are more prone than whites" (2004, p. 42) rather than the result of greater exposure to violence producing social forces. By ignoring the effects of entrenched racial inequality, the culture of individualism encourages these types of explanations and helps to ensure that the mitigating circumstances that are most likely to be present in the lives of poor and minority defendants are precisely the mitigating factors that do not get considered by judges and jurors. As long as cultural discourses play a role in the implementation of capital punishment, guided discretion statutes will remain unable to cure the death penalty of its arbitrary nature.

Implications for Other Social Policies

As a force with deep roots in American culture (Scheingold, 1984), individualism, obviously, affects policies other than the death penalty. Granted the death penalty is an extreme site for studying the impacts of hegemonic individualism, and there are pitfalls with trying to extrapolate from interviews with capital jurors to the larger society. Capital jurors must be death-qualified, and prior research has found such persons are more likely to be conservative, conviction-prone white males who are more punitive than those who are not death-qualified (Fitzgerald and Ellsworth, 1984; Fleury-Steiner, 2004; Haney, 1984; Young, 2004). Therefore, the jurors' reluctance to consider structural mitigation could be an artifact of the death-qualification process. It is possible that those who use macro-level structural theories of human behavior are more likely to be excluded since they may be less likely to support the death penalty in the first place. Therefore, when attempting to determine the hegemonic influence of individualism beyond capital sentencing, the use of death-qualified jurors could be problematic. However, if explicit attempts by the Supreme Court to get sentencers to consider factors beyond individual culpability have not been successful, what does this imply about our ability to solve other social problems? If we cannot acknowledge the important role of social structural factors even when we are directly presented with evidence as to their influence, it seems unlikely that we will be able to devise meaningful social solutions to social problems. In both the United States and United Kingdom, scholars have linked the framing of criminals as individually responsible and wicked plotters unencumbered by social structure and social conditions to a larger conservative agenda to construct a world in which there are winners and losers based solely on individual responsibility (Beckett, 1997; Beckett and Sasson, 2004; Brake and Hale, 1992). In this way, it becomes easier to ignore the social structural conditions that inhibit or enable certain peoples, to believe that "equal protection" laws are enough to combat racial inequality, to blame the poor for their own plight, and to view the luxuries of the wealthy as a just reward for their hard work, determination, or intelligence. This very worldview is at the heart of opposition to social welfare programs, healthcare reform, and affirmative action policies in the United States. As such, viewing the world in this asocial way helps to protect the *status quo* and the privileges of the upper class, insulating them from blame for things such as poverty or racism and from the possibility of redistributive social policies.

For example, individualism teaches Americans that poverty is the result of laziness and irresponsibility rather than blocked opportunities, so providing assistance to the poor is thought to be unfair and unwise. It "steals" money from the rich who "earned" it, and instead of providing needed resources and opportunities, it encourages the poor to remain lazy and unemployed. Considering the highly racialized nature of poverty in America (Brown et al., 2003; Oliver and Shapiro, 1995), there is an undeniable racial element to this image of the poor that is fostered by individualism. Everyone "knows" who the poor are. This knowledge further distances the average American from the poor, who differ not just in class but in race, which makes it easier to blame them for their predicaments and more difficult to get Americans to attend to the real causes of poverty and racial inequality. Thus, the methods utilized to address (or not) issues of race and class inequality are also likely to be influenced by individualism in a manner that affects who receives what benefits and who bears the burdens of those social policies. For example, in the taken-for-granted tale, it makes more sense to lower taxes because this will encourage individuals to work harder since they will see a greater return on their investment than to try stimulating growth by providing funds that would allow the poor to spend more money, thus increasing demand and the need to hire new workers to fill that demand. If such a suggestion is accurate, individualism helps to validate a flawed worldview that places the burdens of inequality and past discrimination on the backs of the poor and minorities while allowing the powerful to maintain their privileged position and unequal access to resources.

This individualistic worldview is not restricted to the United States either. As Brake and Hale (1992) documented in the U.K., a key focus of Thatcher's Conservative government was to shift blame and responsibility back on to individuals in an attempt to dismantle the welfare state. Since "no rational person supports crime," crime and crime control are the perfect vehicles for constructing this hegemonic tale of individual responsibility (Brake and Hale, 1992, p. 37); this remains evident even in the twenty-first century. For example, in a speech about crime, Conservative British politician Michael Howard (2004) argued that the most damaging aspect of society "has been the dramatic decline in personal responsibility. Many people now believe they are no longer wholly responsible for their actions." He continues to argue that "decent, hard-working people" know that the right path for society is "based on personal responsibility, moderation, truthfulness, honesty, and liberty under the law." Howard was attempting to invoke commonsense cultural ideas of individual responsibility in order to shift the role of government from provider to protector from predators. Therefore the findings about individualism's influence on other public policies may have implications for other nations as well.

Theoretical Implications

This study is just a starting point for research into capital mitigation, but it has some important theoretical contributions. The findings show the way one particular cultural narrative (individualism) is filtered through a specific social institution (capital sentencing) in order to create real-world consequences. Culture materially affects they ways in which real human beings are treated. Culture affects lives, and in this case, it can affect who lives. As such, it is important to know how cultural norms affect capital sentencing outcomes and the ways in which courts can either construct or subvert cultural messages.

By following eight capital trials (half of which ended in a life sentence) from the presentation of mitigating evidence to the final sentencing outcome, the study has been able to show that mitigation is significantly more complex and nuanced than the theory of hegemonic individualism would suggest. Yes, the attorneys all presented individualizing accounts of defendants who lacked culpability or who could be sufficiently restrained from killing again by prison, but many also told subversive stories that challenged the core tenets of individualism. They explained how their clients were greatly impacted by forces beyond their control and how they likely would have been significantly different persons had they been given the same opportunities as others. This suggests that there is still a lot to know about mitigation. What evidence do defense attorneys select for presentation and why? What evidence do they reject and why? Is mitigation presented differently in different states or in different parts of the same state? What could be done to improve the presentation of mitigation?

This study also confirms the findings of prior studies that capital jurors are primarily concerned with a defendant's culpability, but through the use of trial transcripts, it is able to offer a preliminary answer as to *why*. This study has shown that defense attorneys do attempt to present contextualizing life history evidence. However, when asked about such evidence, jurors had no recollection of it, dismissed it as irrelevant, or were hostile to it. As such, this study suggests that the reason jurors in prior studies were so concerned with individual culpability was because they rejected the causal significance of external forces. Another possible explanation emerges from the transcripts: perhaps the prosecuting attorneys convinced them not to utilize contextualizing stories, but even if this is the case, the most likely answer for why jurors defaulted to the prosecution's take on the mitigating evidence as an "excuse" rather than the defense's view of the mitigating evidence as an explanation is that culture predisposed the jurors to be skeptical of macro-level theories of social causation.

Lastly, this study brings the decision making of trial judges in capital cases into focus. Judges at this stage had never been subjected to empirical scrutiny. The findings in this study suggest that, like jurors, they too are greatly influenced by the cultural messages of their society. On the one hand, this should not be surprising since judges are humans too and like all other humans, they are impacted by the basic underlying assumptions of their culture. On the other hand, the finding is both surprising and disconcerting. Judges should be quite familiar with Supreme Court case law and so should be better able to apply the law, but the findings in this study suggest that they are not. This conclusion suggests there are limits to the law. If judges cannot shake off the shackles of their culture to apply the law without arbitrariness—and a study by Johnson and her colleagues (2012) suggests that Delaware's death penalty became *more* arbitrary after judges were given final sentencing authority while a study by Givelber and Farrell (2012) suggests that judges overall are less receptive to defense evidence and more racist than jurors are—what hope is there for crafting any sort of capital sentencing statute that eliminates racial discrimination?

This conclusion also supports Gramsci's assertion that courts serve "a repressive and negative educative function" for accomplishing hegemony (1971, p. 258). The death penalty in the United States is more than just a punishment, a method for society to exact vengeance against those who have harmed it or a vain attempt to deter future acts of criminal violence. Capital punishment is an institution for (mis)educating the American public about the nature and origin of human frailties and constructing commonsense narratives focused on individual responsibility in the face of mountains of criminological, sociological, and even psychological evidence that show that human behavior is far more complex than a simple expression of free will. According to Sarat (2001), the death penalty serves the very important function of supporting the individualist ethic. The findings in this research support this claim. In addition to being justified on individualistic logic, the very institution of capital punishment in America creates and constructs individualizing stories of personal responsibility divorced from social context. Even when attorneys attempt to challenge these individualizing stories, they are usually (but not always) met with deaf ears. Far from simply being one of the products of a culture that values individualism, the death penalty is at the heart of constructing the hegemonic tale of taken-for-granted individualism that is rampant in American culture—this is especially true for judicial sentencing opinions, which often serve as the authoritative, impartial source for understanding particular criminal events.

Yet, this study is just a beginning. The small sample size prevents this study from being generalized, but its in-depth narrative analysis provides some important theoretical insights that can be the basis for hypothesis testing in larger, more generalizeable statistical analyses. Do jurors and judges more generally reject contextualizing arguments when forced to confront them? Even beyond capital sentencing, is individualism a paramount factor in support or opposition to other social policies, and can one's degree of adherence to individualistic worldviews explain one's political views? Throughout this book, I have mentioned how individualistic discourses are likely to have a negative impact on minority defendants, but the small sample size of this study did not allow me examine issues of racial or gender bias in any systematic way. Therefore, future studies of mitigation need to analyze all forms of inequality systematically. Does the presentation of mitigation change when the races, classes, or genders of the defendant or victim change, and does the propensity of jurors and judges to dismiss the relevance of structural mitigation—or act hostilely toward it—change when these demographic features change?

Limitations

Before discussing the policy suggestions derived from this research, a note of caution is in order. This is only one study, conducted in one state, with a small sample size. The reasons for this method were explained in Chapter 1, but this method comes with the drawback of not being generalizeable. Although I believe this concern is outweighed by the valuable data that were able to be collected, this limitation does speak to the study's ability to inform public policy debates. Nevertheless, I believe the findings are in line with prior research and existing theory and provide a fruitful avenue for further research to test its claims. Therefore, I feel it is appropriate to offer policy suggestions.

Regarding the use of trial transcripts, it has already been discussed how their inclusion in a study of mitigation and capital sentencing decisions is an analytical advance that helps answer questions as to why decision makers act in the ways that they do. However, transcripts are quite sterile. They are just words on a page. It is impossible for such transcripts to capture the atmosphere of the courtroom, the ways in which attorneys delivered their arguments, or the demeanor of witnesses who testified. Additionally, the actual court exhibits presented to the judge and jury are not included with the transcripts. While the transcripts note what piece of evidence was presented at certain points, the actual reports prepared by experts, the videos and photographs displayed by the attorneys or the defendants' families, and all of the other physical evidence presented in the trial was not available to researchers, but such evidence could certainly have influenced the decisions of judges and jurors. A more comprehensive study of capital mitigation would entail examining all of the court exhibits that were available to the decision makers and attending capital trials to observe and code for things like the body language used by attorneys and witnesses, the words or points they emphasize and the manners in which they emphasize them, the rhythm of their speech, the actual interaction between attorneys and witnesses, the eye contact they each make with the jury, and so on. All of these things may be more important than the actual content of their words and be factored into the decisions jurors and jurists make. Trial transcripts cannot possibly capture all of these additional factors, but attending enough capital trials and coding for all of the non-verbal cues and intonations in lawyers' and witnesses' behavior and speech would be an extremely expensive and time-consuming process that is beyond the scope of this study.

Furthermore, there are limits to the method of interviewing jurors and of reading sentencing opinions. In order to maximize the number of cases with sentencing opinions and court transcripts available for analysis, each of these interviews was conducted five to seven years after the trials were completed. This means that the jurors' memories may have faded, or they may have misremembered or forgotten key facts, such as the defendant's life history. On the one hand, this is beneficial because it helps to isolate what evidence was most memorable and most impacted the jurors. On the other hand, it could lead to faulty conclusions as to the receptivity of jurors to certain pieces of evidence, the importance of certain facts to jurors when making their decisions, and the exact timing of jurors' decisions. However, evidence from the first phase of the CJP suggests that faulty memory is not a serious problem in juror interviews (Bowers and Foglia, 2006).

Additionally, the stories told by capital jurors in *post-hoc* interviews need to be understood as attempts to rationalize and justify their sentencing decisions to an outside interviewer (Fleury-Steiner, 2004, p. 33; Scott and Lyman, 1968). As Fleury-Steiner explains, "Capital jurors' stories can often be heard explicitly as justifications for how and why they made particular decisions. Recounting their experiences, they employ moral justifications as a storytelling technique to persuade the interviewer" (2004, p. 33). Jurors who are being interviewed after they have returned a sentencing recommendation may be searching for acceptable rationales to justify their recommendations rather than accurately recalling what actually influenced their original decisions. The risk of such a justification bias is minimized in this study because I was looking for jurors' use (or lack of use) of legally relevant factors rather than their use of extra-legal variables that they should not have considered and may very well have wished to hide from interviewers and because the interviews indicated that jurors failed to utilize legally relevant variables that they were supposed to be considering. It therefore seems unlikely that the justification bias can account for the responses. Furthermore, there is evidence from the first phase of the CJP that suggests that juror responses are not significantly altered by hindsight bias (Bowers and Foglia, 2007), but even if they are, there is little that can be done to cure this concern unless researchers are permitted to record actual jury deliberations. Otherwise, the only way we can know what evidence influenced jurors is to ask them.

Another important concern regarding this study is that from the data analyzed and presented here, it is not clear whether the jurors' unwillingness to consider life history evidence is the result of their inability to follow the law or the inability of sentencing instructions to clarify what jurors are supposed to do. It is possible that with better jury instructions, capital jurors would consider contextual mitigation, but this seems unlikely. For one, even the judges in this sample, who should be well versed in the law, were reluctant to consider contextual mitigation, so it is hard to imagine how better sentencing instructions could rectify the problem. Secondly, the findings of numerous studies suggest that regardless of what the instructions say, jurors (or mock jurors) do not comprehend mitigation (Bowers, 1996; Haney and Lynch, 1994; Haney and Lynch, 1997; Tiersma, 1995), which suggests that something other than the content of the instructions—such as the culture of individualism—is responsible for the jurors' failure to consider mitigation. Lastly, even if there are flaws in the jury instructions that could be rectified in a way that would encourage considerations of mitigation, these flaws could not have *caused* the jurors to use individualistic theories. They must have defaulted to micro-level explanations for some reason, and the findings of this study are perfectly consistent with the theory that individualism exerts a hegemonic force on jurors that causes them to defer to individualism and to reject theories of external causation.

A final concern regarding the use of juror interviews in Delaware is the fact that Delaware uses an atypical sentencing procedure that may affect juror behavior. For example, Bowers, Foglia, Giles, and Antonio (2006) found that jurors in hybrid sentencing states like Delaware are less likely to take responsibility for their sentencing decisions, and the jurors in this sample also denied responsibility and suggested that they spent little time deliberating the sentence with other jurors (Kleinstuber, 2013). It is possible that by truncating penalty deliberations, this sentencing scheme caused jurors to give less consideration to penalty phase evidence of all kinds, especially contextualizing evidence that challenged their commonsense beliefs. Since the findings regarding the jurors' focus on culpability confirm earlier studies from other states, it does not appear that this is a major concern, but similar studies need to be conducted in other states to verify the findings regarding jurors' rejection of environmental causal forces.

While the use of judicial sentencing opinions to study the influence of mitigating factors on eventual sentences is a huge leap forward, it suffers from its own problems. Judges' sentencing opinions are legal documents in which the judges are trying to justify their sentences to the Delaware Supreme Court. Like the *post-hoc* interviews, judges are writing their sentencing opinions *after* they have decided on a sentence, not while they are deciding, so the opinions cannot possibly capture every factor that went into those decisions. Judges search back through the record or their memories for the most legally pertinent evidence that fits their decision. It is hoped that such factors accurately reflect the factors judges *actually* considered, but there is no way to know that. As Justice Oliver Wendell Holmes (1881) argued more than a century ago, judges make decisions first and then look for formal legal precedents to rationalize those decisions afterward in their written opinions. Since the criminal justice system typically emphasizes individual responsibility, this may have caused jurists to write in individualizing language even if they did consider contextual factors. Therefore, without actually interviewing the judges, it is not known how much the judges were influenced by hegemonic tales. However, as judicial elites, judicial sentencing opinions can be read as a source for constructing cultural narratives. Viewed in this light, what the judges actually thought is not really relevant. What matters are the messages about crime and criminal behavior they are portraying to the public. As an authoritative and supposedly neutral and detached party, the sentencing opinions of judges often serve as a primary source of knowledge about criminal cases, and they are often quoted in newspaper accounts of capital trials. Therefore, the judges' tendency to support or challenge hegemonic understandings of individual responsibility get repeated and conveyed to the public and help to form part of the commonsense understanding of criminality.

Policy Recommendations and the Future of Capital Punishment

There is little in these findings that suggest a possibility for reform. The death penalty seems necessarily influenced by individualism no matter who makes the decision, which suggests that it is not possible to craft sentencing statutes that ensure that all relevant mitigation is considered or that are free of the arbitrariness that has traditionally plagued the death penalty. Legislatures and courts have been toying with the death sentencing process for decades now, yet along with prior scholarship, this research has demonstrated that none of these reforms have led to a more rational or less arbitrary death penalty that is able to consider all relevant factors in a fair and objective manner. Combined with the finding that the prosecutors explicitly tried to get the jurors not to give proper consideration to mitigation and synonymous findings in Texas (Vartkessian, 2011; Vartkessian, 2012), the conclusion that jurors and judges do not consider contextual, environmental factors in their sentencing decisions suggests that no matter what changes are made to the law, it is unlikely that the death penalty can be cured of its arbitrariness. It seems that the death penalty as an institution is destined to discriminate. The discriminatory impact of the death penalty is not isolated to a few states or to a few sentencing statutes. It infects all areas of the United States (Baldus and Woodworth, 2003).

This reality is not necessarily the work of racist judges, jurors, prosecutors, or police. Rather, this research suggests that it is at least partially the result of cultural narratives and prosecutorial strategies that discount the significance of structural factors that disproportionately impact the lives of minorities. Simply put, punishment cannot be divorced from the culture in which it takes place (Garland, 1990). Despite the efforts of the Supreme Court, jurors (and judges) cannot dispense with their cultural baggage when they enter the courtroom. Therefore, they bring with them all of their cultural assumptions and stereotypes, and these get reflected in the way defendants get treated. In other words, racism in the death penalty—like racial inequality more generally—appears to be systemic and therefore incurable by legal changes alone. It is the culture that needs to change—the very culture of individualism that sustains the death penalty's existence to begin with.

Therefore, the findings reported here, in conjunction with the repeated studies on the death penalty's arbitrariness and on juror preoccupation with culpability, suggest that "the death penalty experiment has failed" (*Callins v. Collins*, 1994, p. 1145). In the words of Justice Harry Blackmun, the reality of American death sentencing practices is that we have "a system that we know must wrongly kill some defendants, a system that fails to deliver the fair, consistent, and reliable sentences of death required by the Constitution" (*Callins v. Collins*, 1994, pp. 1145-6). As such, Blackmun's conclusion that we should no longer "tinker with the machinery of death" appears to be accurate. It seems that human beings may be incapable of making the decision to take another person's life in a rational and even-handed manner. Therefore, unless we are prepared to accept a death penalty "that we know must wrongly kill some defendants" and to do so in a racially discriminatory manner, the only truly effective reform would be to abolish capital punishment. Based upon what we know about the punishment's arbitrary operation and what the findings of this project suggest about the power of cultural narratives to prevent decision makers from considering factors that might reduce the penalty's arbitrariness, continuing to use the death penalty itself is an indefensible indication of discriminatory purpose. It is for this reason, perhaps, that six states have abolished the death penalty since 2007 (Death Penalty Information Center, 2013b) and that 17 states, including Delaware, are currently considering possible repeals (Death Penalty Information Center, 2013a).

In a similar vein, the increasing use of LWOP sentences is incredibly concerning. LWOP sentences are not really victories for defendants. The use of LWOP also fails to truly consider contextualizing mitigation. In fact, in their attempts to reassure jurors that it would be okay to sentence the defendant to LWOP, the defense attorneys revealed the problem inherent in LWOP sentences: they are simply less costly death sentences that, ironically, offer convicted killers fewer opportunities to challenge the legality or accuracy of their convictions. As the defense attorneys argued, such sentences are as harsh (or nearly as harsh) as a death sentence and like a death sentence, they ensure that defendants will spend the rest of their lives in a cage. This is an incredibly harsh penalty that also ignores mitigating contextual factors and the realities of entrenched economic, racial, social, and political inequality in American society. If there is to be a true grappling with these cultural pressures and the effects they can have on behavior, then it is imperative to admit that there may be some offenders who, at some point in the distant future, could be effectively rehabilitated and released, which would help reduce prison overcrowding, reduce criminal justice expenditures, and potentially serve the purpose of creating an ex-convict educator who could explain the pitfalls of a violent lifestyle to at-risk youngsters.

Unfortunately, neither the complete abolition of the death penalty nor reductions in the use of LWOP appear imminent. Therefore, in the meantime courts should at least tell prosecutors that while they are allowed to argue that mitigation should not be given much weight or that it does not outweigh aggravation, they are *not* allowed to refer to mitigation as "excuses" or encourage jurors not to consider mitigation *at all.* In *Caldwell v. Mississippi* (1985), the Supreme Court ruled that prosecutors are not allowed to encourage jurors to view themselves as less than fully responsible for the defendant's punishment. Using similar logic, the Court should also tell prosecutors that they cannot tell jurors that contextualizing mitigation is irrelevant; they can attack it, suggest that certain mitigating factors have not been proven to be present, or argue that the mitigators should not carry as much weight as the aggravators, but they should be barred from miseducating jurors about mitigation by suggesting that those mitigators that do exist should be given *no weight.*

There are also steps that defense attorneys can take to combat hegemonic individualism in ways that do not put their clients at greater risk. One trial strategy has already been suggested by Sundby (1997). According to Sundby (1997), incorporating the testimony of lay experts helps provide an unbiased first-hand account that can verify the theories of professional, paid (and presumably biased) mitigation experts. Another strategy that might help jurors take contextualizing life history evidence into account (especially if there is no lay expert available) is to incorporate sociological testimony into the penalty trial. This may be a challenge because evidence typically needs to be shown to be relevant to the specific case at hand, but if jurors are to truly understand why mitigating factors from a defendant's life history are relevant, they may need a crash course in sociology. Psychologists are good because they provide the micro-level framework, and social workers are good because they provide a meso-level analysis of how the defendant was impacted by his immediate environment, but jurors often reject this evidence by suggesting that the defendant could have overcome his environment had he tried hard enough. Therefore, jurors also need a macro-level perspective that can provide them with greater appreciation of the causal significance of social variables. There are social patterns to all behaviors that need explanation beyond just individual free will. Sociological testimony may be able to shed light on this reality by helping jurors to understand that a single or even a few contradictory examples do not shatter a theory because sociological theories are not about showing direct causation. Rather, they are designed to explain social patterns and probabilities. This is the very essence of real mitigation. Mitigation is not about showing inevitability; it is about assessing the formative importance of prior experiences. Having an experienced sociologist, who could testify as to the probabilistic nature of social theories in a manner that would show the jury that the deck was stacked against the defendant in a way that did not guarantee he would lose but that made it far more likely that he would, could be extremely beneficial in getting jurors to recognize the importance of the factual background information provided by other expert witnesses and to consider such evidence in their sentencing deliberations. Perhaps such evidence may also sway judges who lack a sociological background.

In line with this, attorneys should seek ways to address racial inequality when they have minority defendants. Even if race is not a salient issue at trial, it is imperative that attorneys make jurors viscerally aware of the substantial differences between their hardships and the hardships experienced by the defendant (Lyon, 2004). As Lyon (2004) explains, there are ways to do this that would be deemed admissible and would not result in a backlash from the judge or the jury. For example, she suggests setting up a video camera in the defendant's neighborhood and allowing the jurors to watch the disturbing daily trends that characterize such neighborhoods as a means of getting jurors to comprehend the vast social distance between themselves and the defendant. This does not relieve capital defenders assigned the task of defending white defendants of the responsibility to address and combat structural inequality. White defendants' experiences of structural inequality, mistreatment, concentrated disadvantage, and class discrimination are no less real than those of minority defendants (Webster, 2008). It is just that attorneys do not have to travel as far to get (mostly white) jurors to bridge the social divide between themselves and white defendants (Haney, 2004).

Appendix: CJP3 Interview Instrument

As you may remember from our earlier letter to you, this is a project about your experience of serving on a capital trial. In this interview, I'll be asking you first about the crime, including the defendant and the victim; next about the trial, from jury selection to the final jury verdict on punishment, then about your own decision-making, and finally about your experience and impressions as a juror. To prepare for this interview, I reviewed some of the trial transcript to familiarize myself with the case. So, while the purpose of this interview is to gain an understanding of your experience as a juror, there may be time when I ask you for clarifications or elaborations of something that comes from my reading of the transcript.

I. THE CRIME

My first questions are about the crime.

1. When did you first hear about this crime?

___ the same day it occurred
___ a day or two after it occurred
___ a week or two after it occurred
___ a month or more after it occurred
___ not until you were called for jury duty
___ not until after the trial actually began

a. Did you hear or learn details about the crime or the defendant from …

1 yes   2 no

___ friends or neighbors
___ people you know in the criminal justice system
___ newspapers or TV news
___ searching the internet
___ a questionnaire to people who might be selected as jurors
___ other sources, specify

b. From which of these sources did you learn most about the crime or the defendant?

2. Now, I'd like you to tell me about the crime. In your own words, give me the details I need to understand what happened and why.

3. How well do the following words describe the killing?

1 very well **2** fairly well **3** not so well **4** not at all

___ gory
___ vicious
___ calculated
___ cold blooded
___ senseless
___ repulsive
___ the victim(s) was/were made to suffer before death
___ the body(ies) was/were maimed or mangled after death
___ other, specify

4. Is there anything about this crime that sticks in your mind, or that you keep thinking about?

___ no
___ yes; **IF YES,** What is it? Can you tell me why you keep thinking about it?

5. Now, for the record, let me make sure I have some basic facts straight.

a. How many …

#_____ people were killed?
#_____ people were injured, but not killed
#_____ people were responsible for the killing

b. Do you remember the victim's(s') name(s)?
V1 ___________________________
V2 ___________________________
V3 ___________________________

IF MORE THAN ONE, which one did you find most memorable or think most about?

c. Now I'll ask you for some facts about the defendant(s) and victim(s). When you're not sure, give me your best guess and I'll note that you're not sure.

	Defendant(s)			Victim(s)		
	D1	D2	D3	V1	V2	V3
Male/Female	___	___	___	___	___	___
White/Black/ Hispanic/Other	___	___	___	___	___	___
Age (# YRS)	___	___	___	___	___	___
Education (# YRS)	___	___	___	___	___	___
Married/Single	___	___	___	___	___	___
Children (#)	___	___	___	___	___	___
Occupation (when last employed)	___	___	___	___	___	___

6. Were the defendant(s) and victim(s) related in any of the following ways?

1 yes **2** no **3** not sure

___ spouse, ex-spouse (circle which one)
___ other family relations, specify
___ lovers, ex-lovers (circle which one)
___ friends
___ neighbors
___ co-workers
___ employer/employee
___ tenant/landlord
___ acquaintances

___ strangers
___ other relationship, specify

I.A. THE DEFENDANT

Now, I'd like to get your personal impressions of the defendant.

1. To begin with, how would you like me to refer to the defendant in the upcoming questions? By …
   ___ first name
   ___ last name
   ___ Mr. or Ms. with last name
   ___ other specify ___________________

2. Please tell me about (DEFNAME). What kind of person is s/he? I'd like to hear about his/her background, upbringing; character, motives, mental condition; contact and relations with family; peers and associates; history of crime, violence, drug/alcohol use.

3. During the trial, did (DEFNAME) appear to be …

   1 yes, very much **2** yes, somewhat **3** no, not much **4** no, not at all

   ___ uncomfortable or ill at ease
   ___ bored, (i.e., indifferent, remote)
   ___ spruced up to make a good appearance
   ___ frightening, (i.e., threatening, defiant)
   ___ sorry for what s/he had done
   ___ sincere (i.e., honest)
   ___ self confident
   ___ bitter (i.e., resentful)
   ___ showed no emotion whatsoever
   ___ other, specify

4. In your mind, how well do the following words describe (DEFNAME)?

1 very well **2** fairly well **3** not so well **4** not at all

___ from a poor or deprived background
___ a "loner" without many friends
___ doesn't know his/her place in society
___ doesn't know right from wrong
___ has gotten a raw deal in life
___ vicious like a mad animal
___ mentally retarded
___ mentally ill
___ emotionally unstable or disturbed
___ brain damaged
___ dangerous to other people
___ had no sense of regret
___ went out of control when s/he committed the crime
___ sorry for what s/he did
___ showed no emotion
___ resentful, hostile toward authority
___ cold as ice, hard as a stone
___ severely abused as a child
___ raised in a warm loving home
___ someone who loved his/her family
___ someone who lacks a conscience
___ someone who lacks basic human instincts
___ drug addict
___ occasional drug abuser
___ alcoholic
___ occasional alcohol abuser
___ had a history of violence and crime
___ a good person who got off on the wrong foot
___ a good person who just snapped when s/he committed the crime
___ someone who suffered from post-traumatic stress disorder
___ other, specify

I.B. THE VICTIM

Next, I'd like to get your personal impressions of the victim. **[IF THERE WAS MORE THAN ONE],** the one you thought most about or found most memorable

1. First, how would you like me to refer to the victim in the upcoming questions? By …

   ___ first name
   ___ last name
   ___ Mr. or Ms. with last name
   ___ other, specify ________________

2. Please tell me about (VICFNAME). What kind of person was s/he? I'd like to learn about his/her background, upbringing; character, motives, mental condition; contact and relations with family; peers and associates; history of crime, violence, drug/alcohol use.

3. In your mind, how well do the following words describe (VICNAME)?

   1 very well **2** fairly well **3** not so well **4** not at all

   ___ admired or respected in the community
   ___ from a poor or deprived background
   ___ raised in a warm loving home
   ___ someone who loved his/her family
   ___ a "loner" without many friends
   ___ had a wonderful future ahead
   ___ was an innocent or helpless victim
   ___ was emotionally unstable or disturbed
   ___ had a problem with drugs or alcohol
   ___ was too careless or reckless
   ___ anything else, specify

II. THE TRIAL

Now let's talk about the trial, from the selection of the jury through the jury's decision on punishment.

1. How well do you remember each of the following stages of the trial?

   1 very well **2** fairly well **3** not so well **4** not at all

   ___ the selection of the jury

___ hearing evidence about (DEFNAME)'s guilt
___ jury deliberations on (DEFNAME)'s guilt
___ hearing evidence about (DEFNAME)'s punishment
___ jury deliberations on (DEFNAME)'s punishment

II.A. JURY SELECTION

My next questions are about the selection of the jury.

1. Give me your impression of the jury selection process. Was it different from what you expected? In what ways?

2. Were you surprised about …

1 yes 2 no

___ questions you were asked by the prosecutor
___ questions you were asked by the defense attorney
___ questions you were asked by the judge
___ the time it took to select the jury
___ the fact that you were selected for the jury
___ who else was chosen for the jury
___ who got eliminated in the jury selection process

For the things you were surprised about, explain what surprised you.

3. Before jury selection, were you asked to complete a questionnaire …
___ yes, at home before coming to court for jury selection
___ yes, at the courthouse before jury selection began
___ no not asked to complete a questionnaire

IF YES,

a. Were you asked about any of the answers you gave on the questionnaire? What answers were you asked about? Who asked? How did you respond?

4. During jury selection, were you questioned by yourself alone or in a group with others who might serve as the jurors?
   ___ by myself, alone
   ___ in a group with others who might be selected as the jurors
   ___ part of the time alone and part of the time in a group

   a. **IF PART OF THE TIME ALONE AND PART OF THE TIME IN A GROUP,** what questions were you asked when you were alone?

5. Were any of the questions you were asked during jury selection hard for you to answer?
   ___ no
   ___ yes

   a. **IF YES,** which question(s)? Why were they hard? Who asked them? What were your answers?

6. Did you see some people being dismissed from jury service by the judge or eliminated by the prosecution or defense attorneys?
   ___ no
   ___ yes

   a. **IF YES,** what do you remember about the reasons why people were not selected for the jury by the judge or the attorneys?

Let's now talk for a few minutes about the people who were selected for the jury. Here is a list of the 12 jurors (including yourself) to refresh your memory. Hold onto the list of jurors because it may help later on in the interview.

7. Do you remember which juror was selected as the foreman or forewoman?
   juror list # __ was the fore-person

   a. Please explain how he or she was chosen.

8. To the best of your memory, were any of the jurors Blacks, Hispanics, Asians, or other minorities?

___ no
___ yes; **IF SO**, how many were the following minorities
#___ who were Black, African-American:
Juror list #(s) __ __ __ __ __ __
#___ who were Hispanic, Latino:
Juror list #(s) __ __ __ __ __ __
#___ who were Asian:
Juror list #(s) __ __ __ __ __ __
#___ who were other minorities:
Juror list #(s) __ __ __ __ __ __

9. Did you know any of the other jurors by sight or as personal acquaintances before the trial?

___ no
___ yes; **IF SO,** how many did you know before the trial?
___ of personal acquaintances
Juror list #(s) __ __ __ __ __ __
___ known by sight but not personally
Juror list #(s) __ __ __ __ __ __

10. Have you remained in contact with any jurors since the trial was over?

___ no
___ yes; **IF SO,** how many have you stayed in contact with?
___ stayed in contact with
Juror list #(s) __ __ __ __ __ __

11. As the trial was about to begin, were you aware that the jury would decide what the punishment should be if it found the defendant guilty of capital murder?

___ no
___ yes
___ not sure

12. Before we move onto questions about the guilt stage of the trial, were you allowed to go home at all during the trial?

___ no, not after I was selected as a juror
___ no, not after the entire jury was selected
___ yes, between the guilt and penalty stages of the trial
___ yes, on weekends
___ yes, everyday
___ other, (explain)

II.B. GUILT STAGE OF THE TRIAL

Let's now turn to the first part of the trial where you heard evidence about whether or not (DEFNAME) was guilty.

1. What was (DEFNAME)'s main motive for the murder according to the prosecutor?

2. What kinds of evidence did the prosecutor use to link (DEFNAME) to the crime?

1 yes **2** no **3** not sure

___ confession to authorities by (DEFNAME)
___ testimony of an accomplice or co-defendant
___ testimony of a prison inmate who knows (DEFNAME)
___ fingerprint identification
___ blood or hair analysis
___ ballistics tests
___ DNA evidence
___ testimony of a medical or forensic expert
___ testimony of a member of the victim's family
___ photographs of the crime scene
___ photographs of the victim's body showing the manner of the killing (e.g. autopsy photos)
___ other, specify

3. Did any witness for the prosecution other than the police or an accomplice testify that he or she ...

1 yes **2** no **3** not sure

___ actually saw (DEFNAME) commit the crime
___ heard (DEFNAME) admit the crime before s/he was arrested
___ could place (DEFNAME) at the time and place of the crime
___ knew of a motive (DEFNAME) had for the crime
___ heard (DEFNAME) admit the crime after arrested, while awaiting trial

4. Did you find the testimony of any of the witnesses for the prosecution hard to believe?

    ___ no
    ___ yes

    IF SO, which witness(es), what testimony, and why?

5. What were the main reasons why (DEFNAME) should be found not guilty according to the defense?

    1 yes **2** no **3** not sure

    ___ (DEFNAME) had no role whatsoever in the killing
    ___ (DEFNAME) had only a minor role in the killing
    ___ (DEFNAME) killed in self-defense
    ___ (DEFNAME) killed in defense of others
    ___ (DEFNAME) was provoked by the victim or others
    ___ it was an unintentional or impulsive act
    ___ it was an accident or mistake
    ___ (DEFNAME) was mentally retarded and could not fully appreciate the wrongfulness of his/her actions
    ___ (DEFNAME) was mentally ill and could not fully appreciate the wrongfulness of his/her actions
    ___ drugs or alcohol made (DEFNAME) unable to fully appreciate the wrongfulness of his/her actions
    ___ (DEFNAME) was insane
    ___ an accomplice was more to blame
    ___ (DEFNAME) simply was not proved guilty beyond a reasonable doubt
    ___ other, specify ________________

6. Did the defense witnesses include:

    1 yes **2** no **3** not sure

    ___ a forensic expert who challenged the evidence against (DEFNAME)
    ___ a psychologist, psychiatrist, or social worker who testified about (DEFNAME)'s mental condition

___ a witness who challenged the credibility of one or more prosecution witnesses
___ an alibi witness who testified that (DEFNAME) was somewhere else when the crime occurred
___ a member of (DEFNAME)'s family; **IF SO,** What relation to (DEFNAME)?
___ other, specify

7. Did you find the testimony of any of the witnesses for the defense hard to believe?
___ no
___ yes
IF SO, which witness(es), what testimony, and why?

8. Did you find any of the evidence or testimony presented by the prosecution or the defense emotionally difficult to see? or hear?
___ no
___ yes; **IF YES,** what evidence or testimony? How did you handle the emotion in court?

9. Did (DEFNAME) testify at the guilt stage of the trial?
___ no; **IF NO,** what impression did this make on you?
___ yes; **IF SO,** what impression did s/he make on you?

10. After you heard the judge's instructions to the jury for deciding about (DEFNAME)'s guilt, but before you began deliberating with the other jurors, did you then think (DEFNAME) was …
___ guilty of capital murder; that is, murder for which the death penalty could be imposed
___ guilty, but not of capital murder
___ not guilty
___ you were undecided

IF GUILTY OF CAPITAL OR NON-CAPITAL MURDER,

a. How strongly did you think so?

___ absolutely convinced
___ pretty sure
___ not too sure

b. When did you first think so?

c. Why did you first think so?

11. What evidence or testimony was most helpful to you in reaching your final decision on (DEFNAME)'s guilt? Why?

II.C. GUILT DELIBERATIONS

Let's now talk about how the jury decided whether (DEFNAME) was guilty or not guilty of capital murder.

1. About how long did it take the jury to reach its verdict about (DEFNAME)'s guilt?

____# of days; ____# of hours; ____# of minutes

2. In your own words, tell me what the jury did to reach its decision about (DEFNAME)'s guilt? How did the discussion get started; what did different people say; what did they agree and disagree about; how did they finally reach agreement? Start at the beginning and tell me all you can remember. Give me a step-by-step account.

3. During the jury's guilt deliberations, how much did the discussion among the jurors focus on the following topics?

1 great deal **2** fair amount **3** not much **4** not at all

___ (DEFNAME)'s background or upbringing
___ (DEFNAME)'s history of crime and violence
___ (DEFNAME)'s motives or reasons for the crime
___ (DEFNAME)'s role or responsibility in the crime
___ (DEFNAME)'s mental condition or sanity
___ alcohol as a factor in the crime
___ drugs as a factor in the crime
___ (DEFNAME)'s dangerousness if ever back in society
___ pain and suffering of the victim
___ loss and grief of the victim's family
___ brutal or vile manner of the killing
___ believability of certain witnesses
___ role and blameworthiness of an accomplice
___ (DEFNAME)'s appearance or manner in court
___ the ways the attorneys presented their cases
___ jurors' feelings for the family of the victim
___ jurors' feelings toward (DEFNAME)
___ jurors' feelings about the right punishment
___ jurors attitudes about being a "hung jury"
___ the judge's instructions to the jury
___ likelihood that (DEF) would ever be executed
___ how soon (DEFNAME) would get out of prison if not given death
___ the meaning of "proof beyond a reasonable doubt"
___ that (DEFNAME) might be guilty of murder, but not capital murder
___ the possibility that DEFNAME) is altogether innocent, someone else did it

4. What was the single most important factor in the jury's decision about (DEFNAME)'s guilt?

5. Among the topics you did discuss, what were the main areas or points on which jurors disagreed?

6. In deciding guilt, did jurors talk about whether or not (DEFNAME) would, or should, get the death penalty?

___ no
___ yes; **IF SO,** what did they say?

7. During guilt deliberations, did any jurors say they would vote guilty of capital murder but would not vote for the death penalty?

    ___ no
    ___ yes; **IF SO,** please explain

8. Was there any disagreement among the jurors about the meaning of "proof beyond a reasonable doubt?"

    ___ no
    ___ yes; **IF SO,** what did the jurors disagree about; how was it resolved?

9. During your guilt deliberations, did the jury ask the judge any questions?

    ___ no
    ___ yes, **IF SO,** what were the question(s), the judge's response(s), and the jury's reaction(s)?

10. During guilt deliberations …

    a. How many of the jurors would you say talked a lot, how many almost never talked, and how many were between these extremes?

    #___ who talked a lot
    #___ who almost never talked
    #___ who were between these extremes
    (= 12)

    b. Looking now at the list of jurors I handed you earlier, which ones would you say talked a lot?

    talked a lot: Juror list #(s) __ __ __ __ __ __

    c. Which ones were most influential?

    were most influential: Juror list #(s) __ __ __ __ __ __

    d. Were you among ...

    1 yes **2** no **3** not sure

    ___ the most talkative

___ the least talkative
___ the most influential
___ the least influential

11. As best you can remember, how many votes did the jury take to reach its verdict on (DEFNAME)'s guilt?
____ # of votes to reach the guilty verdict

12. About how much time passed before the first jury vote on (DEFNAME)'s guilt was taken?
___ less than 10 minutes
___ 10 to 20 minutes
___ 20 to 40 minutes
___ 40 to 60 minutes
___ 1 to 2 hours
___ more than 2 hours

13. When the first jury vote on the murder charge was taken, how many jurors would you say ...
#_____ voted guilty of capital murder
#_____ voted guilty, but not of capital murder
#_____ voted not guilty
#_____ were undecided
(= 12)

a. How did you vote when the first jury vote on the murder charge was taken?
___ guilty of capital murder
___ guilty, but not of capital murder
___ not guilty
___ undecided

14. What did the jurors most in favor of a capital murder verdict say or do? Did they stick to the same arguments or change their arguments as the deliberations went on? And, who were they on the list of jurors I handed you earlier?
Most in favor of a guilty verdict: Juror list #(s) __ __ __ __ __ __

15. What did the jurors least in favor of a capital murder verdict say or do? Did they stick to the same arguments or change their arguments as the deliberations went on? And, who were they on the list of jurors I handed you earlier?
Least in favor of a guilty verdict: Juror list #(s) __ __ __ __ __ __

16. Were any jurors reluctant to go along with the majority's final vote of guilty on the capital murder charge?

___ no
___ yes;

a. **IF SO,** were you at all reluctant?
___ no
___ yes, **IF SO,** why were you reluctant, why did you join the majority?

17. In your mind, how well do the following words describe the jury during its guilt deliberations?

1 very well **2** fairly well **3** not so well **4** not at all

___ like-minded, saw things the same way
___ close-minded, intolerant of disagreement
___ too quick to make a decision, in a hurry
___ divided, saw things differently
___ disagreeable, unwilling to compromise
___ friendly and respectful to one another
___ dominated by a few strong personalities
___ disrupted by a few troublemakers
___ confused by the judge's instructions
___ made it hard to express yourself
___ paid little attention to what you had to say
___ made you feel like an outsider
___ had their minds made up before deliberating
___ were influenced more by emotions than by facts

18. After the jury found (DEFNAME) guilty of capital murder, but before you heard any evidence or testimony about what the punishment should be, did you then think (DEFNAME) should be given …
___ a death sentence
___ a life sentence
___ undecided

IF A DEATH OR A LIFE SENTENCE,
a. How strongly did you think so?
___ absolutely convinced
___ pretty sure
___ not too sure

b. When did you first think so?

c. Why did you think so?

19. Did you believe that once you had convicted (DEFNAME) of this particular kind of murder, the law of this state made the death penalty ...
    ___ the only acceptable punishment
    ___ the most appropriate punishment
    ___ just one available punishment

20. Can you think of anything more we haven't talked about yet that might help us to understand the jury's guilt decision?

II.D. THE SENTENCING STAGE OF THE TRIAL

Let's turn now to the second part of the trial where the jury had to decide what the punishment should be.

1. In your own words, tell me the main reasons the prosecutor gave for why the jury should sentence (DEFNAME) to death and the main reasons the defense attorney gave for why s/he should be given a life sentence.

2. To the best of your memory, about how many people testified or presented evidence for the prosecution at the punishment stage of the trial?
    _____# testified for the prosecution

3. Did the prosecution witnesses at the punishment stage of the trial include …

    1 yes **2** no **3** not sure

    a ___ an arresting or investigating police officer
    b ___ other law enforcement or corrections personnel
    c ___ a medical or forensic expert
    d ___ a psychologist or psychiatrist
    e ___ others involved as accomplices or co-perpetrators of the crime
    f ___ others involved as witnesses of the crime
    g ___ others involved as victims of the crime
    h ___ persons DEFNAME had harmed or victimized in other crimes

i ___ prison inmates who know (DEFNAME)
j ___ a family or ex-family member of the victim(s)
k ___ a friend or neighbor of the victim(s)
l ___ an employer, co-worker or business acquaintance of the victim(s)
m ___others, specify

4. Now as best you can remember, tell me what the main theme of each witness's testimony was and what you thought about it. Let's start with the prosecution witnesses you remember best.

5. Which witness for the prosecution would you say was most effective and why? Mention any others you thought were especially effective.

6. Did any of the testimony by prosecution witnesses at the punishment stage of the trial "backfire" or actually hurt their case?
___ no
___ yes; **IF SO,** explain

7. How much did the prosecutor's arguments at the punishment stage of the trial emphasize …

1 great deal **2** fair amount **3** not much **4** not at all

___ the death penalty is what (DEFNAME) deserved
___ this is the kind of crime the death penalty is for
___ the death penalty will deter others from killing
___ the death penalty will keep (DEFNAME) from killing again
___ the character and motives of (DEFNAME)
___ past crime or violence of (DEFNAME)
___ drugs as a factor in this crime
___ the brutal or savage character of this crime
___ the reputation and character of the victim(s)
___ the pain and suffering of the victim(s)

___ the loss and grief of victim's(s') family(ies)
___ the punishment wanted by victim's(s') family(ies)
___ (DEFNAME)'s dangerousness to others in prison
___ danger to the public if (DEFNAME) ever escaped or was released from prison
___ how this crime compares to other crimes
___ how (DEFNAME) compares to other criminals

a. What did the prosecutor stress most as the reason why (DEFNAME) should get the death penalty?

Let's now talk about the defense.

8. To the best of your memory, about how many people testified or presented evidence for the defense at the punishment stage of the trial?
_____# testified for the defense

9. Did the defense witnesses at the punishment stage of the trial include ...

1 yes **2** no **3** not sure

a ___ a clergyman who knows (DEFNAME)
b ___ a school teacher of (DEFNAME)
c ___ a social worker or investigator familiar with (DEFNAME)'s background and upbringing
d ___ a medical or forensic expert
e ___ a psychological or psychiatric expert
f ___ an expert on the death penalty
g ___ any others involved in the crime
h ___ spouse or ex spouse of (DEFNAME)
i ___ mother of (DEFNAME)
j ___ father of (DEFNAME)
k ___ brother or sister of (DEFNAME)
l ___ a personal friend of (DEFNAME)
m ___ a neighbor or social acquaintance of (DEFNAME)
n ___ an employer, co-worker or business acquaintance of (DEFNAME)
o ___ others, specify

10. Now as best you can remember, tell me what the main theme of each witness's testimony was and what you thought about it. Let's start with the defense witnesses you remember best.

11. Which witness for the defense would you say was most effective and why? Mention any others you thought were especially effective.

12. Did any of the testimony by defense witnesses at the punishment stage of the trial "backfire" or actually hurt their case?

    ___ no
    ___ yes; **IF SO,** explain

13. How much did the defense attorney's arguments at the punishment stage of the trial emphasize . . .

    1 great deal **2** fair amount **3** not much **4** not at all

    ___ the death penalty is not humane
    ___ the death penalty is not a superior deterrent
    ___ (DEFNAME)'s abuse or mistreatment as a child
    ___ (DEFNAME)'S traumatic life experiences
    ___ the influence of mental illness on (DEFNAME)
    ___ the influence of alcohol on (DEFNAME)
    ___ the influence of drugs on (DEFNAME)
    ___ how factors (DEFNAME) could not control led to the crime
    ___ the recklessness or provocation of the victim(s)
    ___ the major responsibility of others for the crime
    ___ the risk of mistakenly executing the wrong person
    ___ basic human qualities and potential of (DEFNAME)
    ___ (DEFNAME)'s service in the military
    ___ that (DEFNAME) was sorry or asked for mercy
    ___ how (DEFNAME) had changed since this crime
    ___ that (DEFNAME) had become a model prisoner
    ___ that (DEFNAME) had found religion
    ___ the impact (DEFNAME)'s execution would have on his/her loved ones
    ___ how (DEFNAME) or this crime compared to other criminals or crimes

a. What did the defense attorney stress most as the reason why (DEFNAME) should not get the death penalty?

Now let me check the notes I made when I read the trial transcript to see if there were any other defense or prosecution witnesses. It looks like there were a few more we haven't talked about.

For the defense I also have:

____
____
____
____
____

14. Do you remember any of these defense witnesses? Did they say anything that needs to be added to the testimony you have already told me about?

For the prosecution I also have:

____
____
____
____
____

15. Do you remember any of these prosecution witnesses? Did they say anything that needs to be added to the testimony you have already told me about?

16. Did (DEFNAME) testify or make a closing statement at the punishmen stage of the trial?

___ no; **IF NO,** what impression did this make on you?

___ yes, as a sworn witness who could be examined and cross examined by the attorneys

___ yes, though not as a sworn witness, but only to make a closing statement to the jury

IF YES, what impression did this make on you?

17. After hearing all the evidence and the judge's instructions to the jury for deciding on the punishment, but before you began deliberating with the other jurors, did you then think (DEFNAME) should be given …

___ a death sentence
___ a life sentence
___ undecided

IF A DEATH OR A LIFE SENTENCE

a. How strongly did you think so?

___ absolutely convinced
___ pretty sure
___ not too sure

b. When did you first think so?

c. Why did you think so?

18. After hearing all of the evidence, did you believe it proved that …

1 yes **2** no **3** undecided

___ (DEFNAME)'s conduct was heinous, vile or depraved
___ (DEFNAME) would be dangerous in the future

19. After hearing the judge's instructions, did you believe that the law required you to impose a death sentence if the evidence proved that...

1 yes **2** no

___ (DEFNAME)'s conduct was heinous, vile or depraved
___ (DEFNAME) would be dangerous in the future

II.E. SENTENCING DELIBERATIONS

We're now ready to talk about how the jury decided what the defendant's punishment should be.

1. About how long did it take the jury to reach its verdict about (DEFNAME)'s punishment?
   ____# of days; ____# of hours; ____# of minutes

2. In your own words, tell me what the jury did to reach its decision about (DEFNAME)'s punishment. How did the discussion get started; what did different people say; what did they agree and disagree about; how did they finally reach agreement? Start at the beginning and tell me all you can remember. Give me a step by step account.

3. During the jury's punishment deliberations, how much did the discussion among the jurors focus on the following topics?

   1 great deal **2** fair amount **3** not much **4** not at all

___ (DEFNAME)'s background or upbringing
___ (DEFNAME)'s history of crime or violence
___ (DEFNAME)'s role or responsibility in the crime
___ (DEFNAME)'s motive for the crime
___ (DEFNAME)'s planning or premeditation
___ (DEFNAME)'s IQ or intelligence
___ (DEFNAME)'s sorrow or remorse
___ (DEFNAME)'s lack of sorrow or remorse
___ (DEFNAME)'s appearance or manner in court
___ alcohol as a factor in the crime
___ drugs as a factor in the crime
___ mental illness as a factor in the crime
___ insanity as a factor in the crime
___ (DEFNAME)'s dangerousness to others in prison
___ (DEFNAME)'s dangerousness if ever back in society
___ how likely s/he would be to get paroled or pardoned
___ how soon s/he would get a parole or pardon

___ whether or not s/he would ever be executed
___ need to prevent him/her from ever killing again
___ death penalty as a deterrent to killings by others
___ reputation or character of the victim(s)
___ the victim(s)' role or responsibility in the crime
___ innocence or helplessness of the victim(s)
___ pain or suffering of the victim(s) before death
___ loss or grief of victim's(s') family(ies)
___ punishment wanted by victim's(s') family(ies)
___ the way in which the victim(s) was/were killed
___ whether the evidence was strong enough for a capital murder verdict
___ how well the attorneys presented their cases
___ jurors' own attitudes about capital punishment
___ jurors' feelings for the family of the victim
___ jurors' feelings toward (DEFNAME)
___ jurors' feelings toward (DEFNAME)'s family
___ jurors' attitudes about being a "hung jury"
___ what religious beliefs require
___ what moral values require
___ what community feelings require
___ what the law requires
___ that (DEFNAME) committed murder was enough for the death penalty
___ the impact (DEFNAME)'s execution would have on his/her loved ones
___ similarity to other crimes and other murderers

4. What was the single most important factor in the jury's decision about (DEFNAME)'s punishment?

5. During your sentencing deliberations, did the jury stop to ask the judge …

1 yes **2** no

___ for further explanation of the law or clarification of the instructions to the jury
___ for an indication of what would happen if the jury could not reach a decision
___ for a review or transcript of certain testimony
___ for information on how long before (DEFNAME) could be released if not given a death sentence
___ for other information or instructions, specify

a. For each question to the judge, what was the judge's response and what was the jury's reaction?

6. During punishment deliberations:

a. How many of the jurors would you say talked a lot, how many almost never talked, and how many were between these extremes?

___ # who talked a lot
___ # who almost never talked
___ # who were between these extremes
(= 12)

b. Looking now at the list of jurors I handed you earlier, tell me which ones would you say talked the most?

talked the most: Juror list #(s) __ __ __ __ __ __

c. Which ones were most influential?

were most influential: Juror list #(s) __ __ __ __ __ __

d. Were you among …

1 yes **2** no **3** not sure

___ the most talkative
___ the least talkative
___ the most influential
___ the least influential

7. Among the topics you did discuss, during punishment deliberations, what were the main areas or points on which jurors disagreed?

8. Thinking now about the jurors who were most in favor of the death penalty, what did they say or do first, what happened next? Did they stick to the same arguments or change their arguments as the deliberations went on?

a. Who were they on the list of jurors I handed you earlier?

Most in favor: Juror list #(s) __ __ __ __ __ __

9. Thinking about the jurors who were most opposed to the death penalty, what did they say or do first, what happened next? Did they stick to the same arguments or change their arguments as the deliberations went on?

a. Who were they on the list of jurors I handed you earlier?
Most opposed: Juror list #(s) __ __ __ __ __ __

10. As best you can remember, how many votes did it take for the jury to decide what sentence to impose?
____ # of votes to reach the decision on sentence

11. About how much time passed before the first jury vote was taken on what sentence to impose?
___ less than 10 minutes
___ 10 to 20 minutes
___ 20 to 40 minutes
___ 40 to 60 minutes
___ 1 to 2 hours
___ more than 2 hours

12. When the first jury vote was taken, about how many of the jurors …
_____ # voted for a death sentence
_____ # voted for a life sentence
_____ # were undecided
(= 12)

13. Were any jurors reluctant to go along with the majority's final vote on punishment?
___ no
___ yes; **IF SO,**
a. How many were reluctant? Did the differences get resolved?

IF SO, how?

b. Were you at all reluctant?
___ no
___ yes; **IF SO,** why were you reluctant? How did you resolve your reluctance?

14. When the jury took its last vote on punishment, how many jurors …
#___ voted for a death sentence

#___ voted for a life sentence
(=12)

IF THE LAST VOTE THE JURY TOOK WAS NOT UNANIMOUS, how did the jurors decide to end their deliberations?

15. In your mind, how well do the following words describe the jury during its punishment deliberations?

1 very well **2** fairly well **3** not so well **4** not at all

___ like-minded, saw things the same way
___ close-minded, intolerant of disagreement
___ too quick to make a decision, in a hurry
___ divided, saw things differently
___ disagreeable, unwilling to compromise
___ friendly and respectful to one another
___ dominated by a few strong personalities
___ disrupted by a few troublemakers
___ confused by the judge's instructions
___ made it hard to express yourself
___ paid little attention to what you had to say
___ made you feel like an outsider
___ had their minds made up before deliberating
___ were influenced more by emotions than by facts

16. Would you say the judge's sentencing instructions to the jury …

1 yes, very much **2** yes, somewhat **3** no, not much **4** no, not at all

___ simplified the decision-making process
___ confused the decision-making process
___ helped jurors reach agreement
___ actually led to disagreement
___ simply provided a framework for the decision most jurors had already made
___ had little or no influence on the jury's decision

17. Can you think of anything more we haven't talked about yet that might help us to understand the jury's punishment decision?

III. THE JUROR'S OWN SENTENCING DECISION

Now I want to ask you about your own punishment decision.

1. How important were the following considerations for you in deciding on what (DEFNAME)'s punishment should be?

1 very important **2** fairly important **3** not very important **4** not at all important

___ sentences imposed for similar crimes on similar defendants
___ the pain and suffering of the victim(s)
___ the loss and grief of the victim's(s') family(ies)
___ the punishment wanted by the victim's(s') family(ies)
___ (DEFNAME)'s lack of regret for his/her actions
___ the principle of "an eye for an eye"
___ the goal of rehabilitation
___ keeping (DEFNAME) from ever killing again
___ keeping other people from killing
___ lingering doubts that (DEFNAME) was the actual killer
___ lingering doubts that (DEFNAME) should have been convicted of capital murder
___ the vicious or brutal manner of the killing
___ feelings of vengeance or revenge
___ feelings about what moral values require
___ (DEFNAME)'s sorrow or remorse for the crime
___ desire to avoid a horrible mistake
___ desire to avoid deliberately killing someone
___ desire to see justice done
___ weight of aggravating and mitigating factors
___ desire to apply the law correctly
___ desire to see the law enforced
___ community outrage over this crime
___ feelings of compassion or mercy for (DEFNAME)
___ the belief that (DEFNAME) should have a chance to pay for the crime and become a law abiding citizen

2. When you were considering the punishment, did you have any of the following thoughts about (DEFNAME)'s guilt; that s/he …

1 yes, very much **2** yes, somewhat **3** no, not much **4** no, not at all

___ might be altogether innocent, a case of mistaken identity

___ definitely had planned or intended to kill the victim, but might not be the one who did so
___ definitely killed the victim, but might not have planned, intended, or wanted to do so
___ might not be the one most responsible for the killing

3. When you were considering the punishment, did you believe that (DEFNAME) was truly sorry for the crime?
___ yes, sure (DEFNAME) was sorry
___ yes, think (DEFNAME) was sorry
___ not sure, (DEFNAME) acted sorry but it might have been a show
___ no, (DEFNAME) acted sorry but it was just a show
___ no, (DEFNAME) didn't even pretend to be sorry

4. When you were considering the punishment, were you concerned that (DEFNAME) might get back into society someday, if not given the death penalty?
___ yes, greatly concerned
___ yes, somewhat concerned
___ yes, but only slightly concerned
___ no, not at all concerned

5. How likely did you think it was that (DEFNAME) would:

1 very likely **2** likely **3** 50-50 chance **4** unlikely **5** very unlikely

___ kill again if let out of prison
___ kill again in prison
___ commit a violent criminal act of any kind if let out of prison
___ commit a violent criminal act of any kind in prison
___ try to get revenge against members of the jury if let out of prison

6. How long did you think someone not given the death penalty for a capital murder in this state usually spends in prison?
______ # of years

7. How much was your belief about the time capital murderers not sentenced to death usually stay in prison based on the following sources?

1 great deal **2** fair amount **3** not much **4** not at all

___ friends and neighbors
___ people you know in the criminal justice system
___ newspapers or TV news

___ TV crime shows, like Crime Scene Investigation (CSI), Law & Order, and others
___ the judge in this case
___ the prosecutor in this case
___ the defense attorney in this case
___ other members of this jury, **IF SO,** which ones?

8. When you were considering the punishment, did you think that whether (DEFNAME) lived or died was …
    ___ strictly the jury's responsibility and no one else's
    ___ partly the jury's responsibility and partly the responsibility of the judge and appeals courts who review the jury's sentence
    ___ mostly the responsibility of the judge and appeals courts; we make the first decision but they make the final decision

9. Did the chance that your punishment decision might be overruled or changed by an appeals court make you feel …

    1 yes **2** no **3** not sure

    ___ good, because you would not have the death of another human being on your conscience
    ___ good, because it meant that any mistakes we might have made could be corrected
    ___ bad, because it means our sentencing decision was less important
    ___ bad, because it means that (DEFNAME) might not get what s/he deserves

10. Rank the following from "most" through "least" responsible for (DEFNAME)'s punishment.

    Give 1 for most responsible through 5 for least responsible

    ___ the law that states what punishment applies
    ___ the judge who imposes the sentence
    ___ the jury that votes for the sentence
    ___ the individual juror since the jury's decision depends on the vote of each juror
    ___ (DEFNAME) because his/her conduct is what actually determined the punishment

11. How well do the following statements describe the way you made your punishment decision?

1 very well **2** fairly well **3** not so well **4** not at all

___ found a specific feature or aspect of the case that made you feel you knew whether life or death should be the punishment
___ used the evidence to develop your own "story" about what happened, and why, that made you feel you knew what the punishment should be
___ thought about the factors for and against a death sentence and then "weighed" one side against the other
___ made your guilt and punishment decisions together on the basis of similar considerations
___ made your guilt and punishment decisions separately on the basis of different considerations

12. Of the following considerations, identify the three most important to you in making your punishment decision.

1 most important **2** second most important **3** third most important

___ the nature and circumstances of the crime
___ the background and character of the defendant
___ his/her danger to society if not given the death penalty
___ the desire to avoid making a mistake
___ the desire to show others how we feel about such crime
___ the desire to do what the laws of this state require
___ the desire to do what moral values require

13. What evidence or testimony was most helpful to you in reaching your punishment decision? Why? Please explain.

14. Did you find any of this evidence or testimony emotionally difficult to see or hear?

___ no
___ yes; **IF YES**, what evidence or testimony? How did you handle the emotion in court?

15. How much was your thinking about (DEFNAME)'s punishment influenced by other jurors' ...

1 great deal **2** fair amount **3** not much **4** not at all

___ insights about (DEFNAME)'s motives
___ insights about (DEFNAME)'s character
___ knowledge about the law or legal issues
___ knowledge of time served by persons not sentenced to death
___ knowledge about factors involved in the crime like the weapon, the effect of drugs, medical facts
___ insights about the victim's(s') character or role in the crime
___ views and feelings about (DEFNAME)'s punishment
___ other issues or topics, specify

16. Which other jurors most influenced your thinking about what (DEFNAME)'s punishment should be? Who influenced you most? Mention any others who also influenced you.
   From most to less influenced you: Juror list #'s __ __ __ __ __ __

17. How did you vote …
   a. At the first jury vote on (DEFNAME)'s punishment
      ____ for a death sentence
      ____ for a life sentence
      ____ undecided

   b. At the final vote on (DEFNAME)'s punishment?
      ____ for a death sentence
      ____ for a life sentence

   c. **IF FIRST AND FINAL VOTES ARE NOT THE SAME,** what caused you to change your mind?

III.A. SENTENCING CONSIDERATIONS

Some things about a murder, the victim, or the defendant, make people feel that a death sentence should or should not be imposed.

1. I am going to read you a list of things that might occur in a murder case. For each one, please tell me first whether it came up in the (DEFNAME) case, and whether you believed it. If so, I then want you to tell me whether it made you …

1. much more likely to vote for death
2. slightly more likely to vote for death
3. slightly less likely to vote for death
4. much less likely to vote for death
5. not more or less likely to vote for death
6. it never came up in this case
7. it came up but I didn't believe it

a. First are factors about the killing:
___ the killing was committed during another crime, such as a robbery, when the victim tried to resist
___ the killing was planned ahead of time
___ the killing was not premeditated or planned ahead of time
___the killing was especially bloody or gory
___the killing was brutal, involving torture or physical abuse
___the killing was a senseless act of violence
___it was committed while (DEFNAME) was under the influence of alcohol
___it was committed while (DEFNAME) was under the influence of drugs
___it was committed while (DEFNAME) was under the influence of an extreme mental or emotional disturbance
___ (DEFNAME) made the victim suffer before death
___ (DEFNAME) maimed or mutilated the victim's body after death
___this crime was out of character for (DEFNAME)

b. Next are factors about the victim:
___the victim was a female
___the victim was young
___the victim was innocent or helpless
___the victim was a respected person in the community
___the victim was a stranger in the community
___the victim was a known troublemaker
___the victim had a criminal record
___the victim was an alcoholic
___the victim was a drug addict
___the victim had a loving family

c. Next are factors about the defendant:
___ (DEFNAME) had no previous criminal record

___ (DEFNAME) had a criminal record but not including violent crime
___ (DEFNAME) had a history of violent crime
___ (DEFNAME) was mentally retarded
___as a child (DEFNAME) had a loving family
___as a youth (DEFNAME) was well behaved in school
___ (DEFNAME) was young when the crime occurred
___ (DEFNAME) was an alcoholic
___ (DEFNAME) was a drug addict
___ (DEFNAME) had a history of mental illness
___ (DEFNAME) had a background of extreme poverty
___ (DEFNAME) was a stranger in the community
___ (DEFNAME) had been physically abused as a child
___ (DEFNAME) had been sexually abused as a child
___ (DEFNAME) had been mentally or psychologically abused as a child
___ (DEFNAME) got no real help or treatment for his problems in the past
___ (DEFNAME) was trying to better him/her self while in prison
___ (DEFNAME) became religious while in prison
___ (DEFNAME) would be a well behaved inmate
___ (DEFNAME) would be a danger to society in the future
___ (DEFNAME) would be a danger to others in prison
___ (DEFNAME) would not be a danger in the future
___ (DEFNAME) expressed remorse, regret or sorrow for the crime
___ (DEFNAME) did not show remorse, regret or sorrow for the crime
___ (DEFNAME) accepted full responsibility for his/her actions
___ (DEFNAME) had a good record of military service
___ (DEFNAME) suffered from post-traumatic stress disorder

d. Additional factors that might have affected your sentencing decision:

___ (DEFNAME) was convicted with evidence from an accomplice who testified against him/her
___the victim's family suffered severe loss or grief
___the death penalty would provide closure for the victim's family
___ (DEFNAME)'S family was partly responsible for the crime
___ (DEFNAME)'S execution would cause his/her family severe loss or grief
___the community was outraged over the crime
___most community members wanted the death penalty
___although the evidence was sufficient for a capital murder conviction, you had some lingering doubt that (DEFNAME) was the actual killer
___in light of the evidence, you had some lingering doubt that (DEFNAME) should have been convicted of capital murder

___ (DEFNAME) did not testify on his/her own behalf

If there are other factors not on this list that affected your sentencing decision, please tell me what they are, and whether they made you more or less likely to vote for a death sentence.

III.B. SENTENCING GUIDELINES

Let's take a minute or two to talk about the judge's instructions to the jury for deciding what the punishment should be. I'll start with a general question.

1. Did you have any difficulty understanding or following the judge's sentencing instructions to the jury?
   ___ no
   ___ yes; **IF SO,** explain

2. Did the judge use the words "aggravating" or "mitigating" factors in his or her sentencing instructions to the jury?
   ___ no
   ___ not sure
   ___ yes; **IF YES,** what did you understand these terms to mean?

Now I have some more specific questions about how jurors may make their sentencing decisions

3. For a factor in favor of a death sentence to be considered, did it have to be …
   ___ proved beyond a reasonable doubt
   ___ proved by a preponderance of the evidence
   ___ proved only to a juror's personal satisfaction
   ___ don't know

4. For a factor in favor of a death sentence to be considered, did …
   ___ all jurors have to agree on that factor
   ___ jurors not have to agree unanimously on that factor
   ___ don't know

5. Among factors in favor of a death sentence, could jurors consider …
   ___ any factor that made the crime worse

___ only a specific list of factors mentioned by the judge
___ don't know

6. For a factor in favor of a life sentence to be considered, did it have to be …
___ proved beyond a reasonable doubt
___ proved by a preponderance of the evidence
___ proved only to a juror's personal satisfaction
___ don't know

7. For a factor in favor of a life sentence to be considered, did …
___ all jurors have to agree on that factor
___ jurors did not have to agree unanimously on that factor
___ don't know

8. Among factors in favor of a life sentence, could jurors consider …
___ any factor in favor of a life sentence
___ only a specific list of factors mentioned by the judge
___ don't know

IV. EXPERIENCE AS A JUROR

We are now ready to talk about your personal reaction to serving as a juror on the (DEFNAME) case. We turn first to your impressions of the prosecuting and defense attorneys.

IV.A. IMPRESSIONS OF THE PROSECUTION, DEFENSE AND JUDGE

1. For the prosecution, how many attorneys were involved?
_____ # of prosecuting attorneys

a. **IF MORE THAN ONE,** how did they allocate the work?
___ one took primary responsibility throughout the trial
___ they shared responsibility for presenting evidence throughout the trial
___ they divided responsibility; one handled the guilt portion and another handled the punishment portion of the trial

2. Give me your impression of the prosecutor. What was s/he like? What was your first impression, how did it change over the course of the trial? What did you think was most and least effective about his/her performance? Did s/he have any irritating or endearing mannerisms?

3. For the defense, how many attorneys were involved?
   _____ # of defense attorneys

   a. **IF MORE THAN ONE,** how did they allocate the work?
      ___ one took primary responsibility throughout the trial
      ___ they shared responsibility for presenting evidence throughout the trial
      ___ they divided responsibility; one handled the guilt portion and another handled the punishment portion of the trial

4. Give me your impression of the defense attorney. What was s/he like? What was your first impression, how did it change over the course of the trial? What did you think was most and least effective about his/her performance? Did s/he have any irritating or endearing mannerisms?

5. How did the defense attorney(s) treat (DEFNAME) during the trial?
   ___ acted like (DEFNAME) wasn't even there
   ___ occasionally spoke to (DEFNAME) but mostly ignored him or her
   ___ frequently talked to (DEFNAME) but didn't seem to involve him or her in their decisions
   ___ seemed to have a close working relationship with (DEFNAME) as part of the defense team

6. Now, I would like you to rate the prosecution and the defense by indicating the extent of your agreement or disagreement with the following statements. Use a scale from 10 to 0, where *10 means you "absolutely agree, 0 means you absolutely disagree, and 5 means you neither agree nor disagree*" with the statement as it applies to the prosecution or defense.

Prosecution Rating	Defense Rating	
__	__	was effective in communicating with the jury
__	__	had money and resources to work with
__	__	prepared their case well for the guilt trial
__	__	prepared their case well for the punishment trial
__	__	fought hard at the guilt stage of the trial
__	__	fought hard at the punishment stage of the trial
__	__	cared more about winning than seeing justice done
__	__	was warm and friendly toward (DEFNAME)
__	__	was hostile toward (DEFNAME)
__	__	was competent and professional

__ | __ was someone you did not like personally
__ | __ was someone who won your respect or admiration

7. Now, give me your impression of the judge. What was s/he like? What was your first impression, how did it change over the course of the trial? What did you think was most and least effective about his/her performance? Did s/he have any irritating or endearing mannerisms?

8. How do you feel about the role the jury foreperson played during the jury's deliberations on punishment? How well do the following characterize him or her?

1 very well **2** fairly well **3** not so well **4** not at all

___ take charge style
___ laid back style
___ strict on rules about talking and taking turns
___ respectful of all jurors' opinions and right to express themselves
___ favored some jurors over others
___ tried to move opinion his or her way

a. Did the same person serve as foreperson at both stages of the trial?
___ yes
___ no; **IF NO**, How and why did the change of foreperson come about, and which juror was foreperson for penalty deliberations?

RECORD jury list # __

IV.B. PERSPECTIVE ON THE DEFENDANT AND THE VICTIM

We previously discussed the defendant and victim; now I'd like to ask you about your more personal reactions to these individuals and their families.

1. Did (DEFNAME) remind you of someone or make you think about anyone?
___ no
___ yes; **IF SO,** who? Describe the person(s).

2. Did you have any of the following thoughts or feelings about (DEFNAME) during the trial?

1 yes, very much **2** yes, somewhat **3** no, not much **4** no, not at all

___ imagined yourself in (DEFNAME)'s situation
___ found (DEFNAME) frightening to be near
___ felt anger or rage toward (DEFNAME)
___ felt pity or sympathy for (DEFNAME)
___ found (DEFNAME) likable as a person
___ was disgusted or repulsed by (DEFNAME)
___ sometimes couldn't stand to look at (DEFNAME)
___ imagined being like (DEFNAME)
___ other reactions, specify

3. Did any of (DEFNAME)'s family members come to the trial?
___ no, I am sure they did not
___ no, I don't think so
___ yes, I think so
___ yes, I am sure they did

IF YES,

a. Which family member(s) do you think/are sure were at the trial:

b. Did any member of (DEFNAME)'s family remind you of someone or make you think about anyone?
___ no
___ yes; **IF SO,** who? Describe the person(s).

4. Whether or not they came to the trial, did you have any of the following thoughts or feelings about (DEFNAME)'s family?

1 yes, very much **2** yes, somewhat **3** no, not much **4** no, not at all

___ imagined yourself in their situation

___ imagined yourself as a member of (DEFNAME)'s family
___ felt anger or rage toward (DEFNAME)'s family
___ felt contempt or hatred for (DEFNAME)'s family
___ felt sympathy or pity for (DEFNAME)'s family
___ felt they seemed very different from your own family
___ wished you knew (DEFNAME)'s family personally
___ felt they were partly to blame for what happened

5. Did (DEFNAME)'s mood or attitude change after the guilty verdict was handed down and the trial shifted to what the punishment should be?
___ no
___ yes; **IF SO,** how?

6. Give me any final thoughts or observations you may have about (DEFNAME) or his family.

Now, let's talk briefly about the (VICNAME) and his/her family. Again, I will ask you about your more personal feelings and reactions.

7. Did (VICNAME) remind you of someone or make you think about anyone?
___ no
___ yes; **IF SO,** who? Describe the person(s).

8. Did you have any of the following thoughts or feelings about (VICNAME)?

1 yes, very much **2** yes, somewhat **3** no, not much **4** no, not at all

___ admired or respected (VICNAME)
___ imagined yourself in (VICNAME)'s situation
___ imagined yourself as a friend of (VICNAME)
___ imagined (VICNAME) as a member of your own family
___ felt grief or pity for (VICNAME)
___ were disgusted or repulsed by (VICNAME)
___ wished (VICNAME) had been more careful
___ imagined being like (VICNAME)

___ other reactions, specify

9. Did any of (VICNAME)'s family members come to the trial?
   ___ no, I am sure they did not
   ___ no, I don't think so
   ___ yes, I think so
   ___ yes, I am sure

   a. **IF YES,** which family member(s) you think/are sure were at the trial:

   b. **IF YES,** did any member of (VICNAME)'s family remind you of someone or make you think about anyone?
      ___ no
      ___ yes; **IF SO,** who? Describe the person(s)

10. Whether or not they came to the trial, did you have any of the following thoughts or feelings about (VICNAME)'s family?

    1 yes, very much **2** yes, somewhat **3** no, not much **4** no, not at all

    ___ imagined yourself in their situation
    ___ felt sympathy or pity for them
    ___ felt their grief and sense of loss
    ___ felt distant or remote from them
    ___ felt they were partly to blame for what happened
    ___ felt they seemed very different from your own family
    ___ wished you knew (VICNAME)'s family personally
    ___ imagined yourself as a member of (VICNAME)'s family

11. Give me any final thoughts or observations you may have about (VICNAME) or his/her family.

IV.C. OPINIONS ABOUT CRIME AND JUSTICE

Here I'll be asking for your opinions about the criminal justice process. I begin with a question about the criminal justice process and then move to a few questions more specifically about capital punishment.

1. How strongly do you agree or disagree with the following statements about the criminal justice process?

1 strongly agree **2** agree **3** not sure **4** disagree **5** strongly disagree

Now Before serving on the (DEFNAME) case

___ | ___ it is better for society to let some guilty people go free than to risk convicting an innocent person
___ | ___ if we really cared about crime victims, we would make sure that criminals were given harsh punishments
___ | ___ if we really cared about crime victims, we would make offenders work to pay for the injuries and losses of their victims
___ | ___ if the police obtain evidence illegally, it should not be allowed in court, even if it would help convict a guilty person
___ | ___ the insanity plea is a loophole that allows too many guilty people to go free
___ | ___ a person on trial who does not take the witness stand and deny the crime is probably guilty
___ | ___ prosecutors have to be watched carefully, since they will use any means they can to get convictions
___ | ___ defense attorneys have to be watched carefully since they will use any means to get their clients off
___ | ___ jurors too often rely upon their personal biases when making their decisions
___ | ___ jurors too often have their minds made up before considering all the evidence
___ | ___ female jurors are too easily distracted by emotions
___ | ___ male jurors are too sure they are right
___ | ___ minority jurors should always be on juries in cases with a minority defendant
___ | ___ minority jurors should always be on juries in cases with a minority victim

a. Were any of your views different before you served as a juror on the (DEFNAME) trial? I'll go back over these statements and where your views have changed, indicate your level of agreement before the (DEFNAME) trial.

2. How strongly do you agree or disagree with the following statements about punishment for convicted murderers?

1 strongly agree **2** agree **3** not sure **4** disagree **5** strongly disagree

Now	Before serving on this case	
___	___	you wish we had a better way than the death penalty of punishing murderers
___	___	the death penalty is too arbitrary because some people are executed while others serve prison terms for the same crimes
___	___	if the death penalty were enforced more often there would be fewer murders in this country
___	___	even convicted murderers should not be denied hope of parole some day, if they make a real effort to pay for their crimes
___	___	defendants who can afford good lawyers almost never get a death sentence
___	___	the death penalty should be required when someone is convicted of a serious intentional murder
___	___	you have moral doubts about death as punishment
___	___	persons sentenced to prison for murder in this state are back on the streets far too soon
___	___	an innocent person has been executed within the past five years
___	___	most people sentenced to death in this state are never executed
___	___	the cost of the death penalty to taxpayers is too great

a. Were any of your views different before you served as a juror on the (DEFNAME) Trial? I'll go back over the statements and where your views have changed, indicate your level of agreement before the (DEFNAME) trial.

3. Do you feel that the death penalty is the only acceptable punishment, an unacceptable punishment, or sometimes acceptable as punishment for the following specific kinds of murder?

1 only acceptable **2** sometimes acceptable **3** unacceptable

___ a planned, premeditated murder
___ a killing that occurs during another crime
___ murders in which more than one victim is killed
___ murder by someone previously convicted of murder
___ murder by a drug dealer
___ killing of a police officer
___ killing of a prison guard

4. Do you now generally favor or oppose the death penalty for convicted murderers?
    ___ strongly favor
    ___ somewhat favor
    ___ somewhat oppose
    ___ strongly oppose
    ___ not sure; don't know

5. For convicted murders, do you now personally prefer …
    ___ life in prison without the possibility of parole
    ___ the death penalty
    ___ not sure; don't know

6. How have your views about the death penalty changed as a result of serving as a juror on the (DEFNAME) case?

IV.D. REACTIONS TO THIS CASE

1. Did you find the experience of serving as a juror on the (DEFNAME) case emotionally upsetting?
    ___ no
    ___ yes; **IF SO,** in what ways?

2. During the trial or right after it, did you have any trouble sleeping, any bad dreams or nightmares, or lose your appetite?
    ___ no
    ___ yes; **IF SO,** explain or elaborate.

3. When you think back about serving as a juror on the (DEFNAME) case, is there anything you wish you had said or done differently?
    ___ no
    ___ yes; **IF SO,** what was it? Anything else?

4. How would you feel if you were asked to serve as a juror on another death penalty case? Would you …

___ welcome the opportunity
___ do so reluctantly
___ try to get out of it
___ refuse to do so

5. How much have you talked about the experience of serving as a juror on the (DEFNAME) case to others including …?

1 great deal **2** fair amount **3** not much **4** not at all

___ friends
___ neighbors
___ husband or wife
___ other family members
___ reporters, journalists, or other people from the media
___ the prosecutor or someone from his/her office
___ the defense attorney or someone from his/her office
___ the trial judge
___ other jurors on the (DEFNAME) case after the trial was over
___ a counselor or therapist
___ other people, specify

a. Did you find it difficult or awkward to talk about serving as a juror on the (DEFNAME) case with any of those you talk to about it?
___ no
___ yes; **IF YES,** please explain

6. How disturbing did you find the following things about serving as a juror at the (DEFNAME) trial … ?

1 very disturbing **2** somewhat disturbing **3** not very disturbing
4 not at all disturbing

___ the prosecuting attorney's behavior during the trial
___ the defense attorney's behavior during the trial
___ difficulty understanding and following the judge's instructions

___ difficulty understanding complex or technical evidence (e.g., expert testimony)
___ grisly photographs or videos presented as evidence (e.g., pictures of victims, crime scene, surveillance tapes, etc.)
___ the victim's family's testimony during the sentencing phase
___ the defendant's family's testimony during the sentencing phase
___ the jury selection process (e.g., answering personal questions in front of other people)
___ the overall length of the trial, not including deliberations
___ the length of the deliberations
___ trial interruptions or delays
___ troubles at home or work during jury duty
___ publicity and media coverage about the trial
___ being publicly identified as a juror
___ menacing behavior by the defendant (e.g., staring, gestures, etc.)
___ fear of reprisal or concerns for your own safety
___ not being able to discuss the case with others outside the jury
___ not being able to discuss the case with other jurors until deliberations
___ having limited input during the trial; not being allowed to ask questions
___ overall lack of legal guidance

7. In your opinion, how helpful would the following be to jurors in making their punishment decisions …

1 very helpful **2** fairly helpful **3** not helpful **4** unhelpful

___ be informed of how likely it would be that a jury decision for the death penalty would be accepted or rejected by the trial judge?
___ be informed of how likely it was that a death sentence would be accepted or rejected by an appeals court?
___ allow jurors to ask for clarification when they don't understand something the judge, attorneys, or witnesses said
___ allow jurors to ask the defendant questions if he testifies by raising their hands or by passing questions they have to the judge who will read them aloud
___ allow jurors to take notes during the trial testimony so they can have a clear record of what was said and what they thought about it
___ be told how long a murderer not sentenced to death would spend in prison before first becoming eligible for parole
___ be told how long it usually takes a murderer not sentenced to death to get parole after first becoming eligible
___ make the trial transcript available to jurors when they first sit down to make their punishment decision

___ videotape jury deliberations so that a complete record of the decision process is available to the judge and appeals courts so it can be examined for any mistakes or departures from legal requirements

a. Were any of these helpful in (DEFNAME) case? **IF SO**, which ones?

8. What further thoughts or recommendations do you have about how to improve the experience and performance of jurors on capital cases?

V. PERSONAL BACKGROUND

Lastly, I need to ask you a few questions about yourself.

1. Are you:

a.

____ male
____ female

b.

____ White
____ Black, African American
____ Hispanic, Latino
____ Asian
____ other

2. What was your age at your last birthday?

______# years old

3. Are you:

___ single, never been married
____ married and living with your spouse
____ married but separated
____ divorced
____ widowed

4. Do you have any children, step children or foster children; **IF SO,** what is the age and sex of each?

RECORD AGE (# YRS) AND SEX (M OR F) OF EACH

___ no children
___ yes, your own ____ ____ ____ ____ ____ ____ ____ ____
___ yes, step ____ ____ ____ ____ ____ ____ ____ ____
___ yes, foster ____ ____ ____ ____ ____ ____ ____ ____

a. **IF YES,** which, if any, are now living with you?

5. What was the last grade of school you completed?
____ grades completed
____ finished high school
____ some technical school beyond high school
____ some college but did not graduate
____ graduated from college
____ graduate or professional school

6. Are you currently employed outside of the home?
___ yes, full-time
___ yes, part-time
___ no, housewife, homemaker, child rearing
___ no, injury, disability
___ no, layoff, strike
___ no, student
___ no, retired
___ no, without explanation

IF EVER EMPLOYED,
a. What kind of work do (or did) you do?

b. What job or position do (or did) you have?

7. Roughly speaking, in which of the following categories does your current family income fall?
___ less than $10,000 a year
___ $10,000-$20,000 a year
___ $20,000-$30,000 a year

___ $30,000-$50,000 a year
___ $50,000-$75,000 a year
___ $75,000-$100,000 a year
___ more than $100,000 a year

8. How would you describe yourself politically?
___ very conservative
___ fairly conservative
___ moderate, middle of the road
___ fairly liberal
___ very liberal
___ don't know, not political

9. Are you involved in any of the following groups or organizations?

1 yes **2** no

___ school or parent/teacher association
___ youth activities, e.g., Little League, Boy Scouts
___ political parties, candidates or campaigns
___ church or religious groups
___ special interest groups, e.g., Sierra Club, NRA, Please specify

IF ANY SUCH INVOLVEMENTS, have you held office or taken a leadership role? Explain.

10. What do you like most to do for recreation?

11. What is your religious preference?
___ Baptist
___ Southern Baptist
___ Lutheran
___ Methodist
___ Presbyterian
___ Evangelical
___ Protestant, specify
___ Roman Catholic
___ Jewish
___ Other religion, specify

___ No religious preference

12. How often do you attend religious services?

___ more than once a week
___ once a week
___ several times a month
___ once a month
___ several times a year
___ once a year, or less
___ never

13. Did your religious beliefs have any impact on your decision in the (DEFNAME)'s case?

___ no
___ yes; **IF SO,** what was the impact?

14. Have you served in the military?

___ no
___ yes; **IF SO,** what branch and what was the nature of your service?

15. How long have you lived at your current address?

_____ # of years;

16. Do you rent or own your own home?

___ rent
___ own

Concerning your previous experience with the criminal justice system …

17. Did you serve on a trial jury before this case?

___ no
___ yes, on a criminal case
___ yes, on a civil case

18. Did you ever attend a criminal trial in some other capacity before this case?

___ no
___ yes; **IF SO,** ___ as a spectator
___ as a witness

___ as a defendant

19. Have you or other members of your household been the victim of a serious crime in the past five years

___ no
___ yes; **IF YES,** what was the nature of the most serious crime, and did it happen before or after (DEFNAME)'s trial?

20. Do you know people who work in the law enforcement or criminal justice fields?

1 yes **2** no

___ in the police, including private security
___ in the courts, including judges, prosecutors, defense attorneys, clerks or other staff
___ in corrections, including jails, prisons or other corrections facilities

21. Have you ever worked or held a position in law enforcement corrections, or criminal justice?

___ no
___ yes; **IF YES,** please provide details.

22. Do you watch any of the CSI or crime investigation type TV shows?

___ no
___ yes; **IF YES ...**

a. Which shows?

b. How did the presentation of forensic evidence in (DEFNAME)'S case compare to what is presented in those shows?

23. Have you been interviewed by anyone else, attorneys, investigators, media etc. about your experience as a juror on this case?
    ___ no
    ___ yes; **IF SO,** explain.

Thank you very much for your cooperation.

References

Abdul-Kabir v. Quarterman, 550 U.S. 233 (2007).

American Bar Association, 2003. *Guidelines for the Appointment and Performance of Defense Counsel in Death Penalty Cases, revised edition.* Chicago(IL): ABA.

American Bar Association, 2008. Supplementary Guidelines for the Mitigation Function of Defense Teams in Death Penalty Cases. *Hofstra Law Review*, Volume 36, pp. 677-92.

American Judicature Society, 2012. *Judicial Selection in the States.* [Online] Available at: http://www.judicialselection.us/judicial_selection/index.cfm [Accessed 6 August 2012].

Anderson, E., 1999. *Code of the Street: Decency, Violence, and the Moral Life of the Inner City.* New York: W.W. Norton.

Baldus, D.C., Pulaski, C., and Woodworth, G., 1983. Comparative Review of Death Sentences: An Empirical Study of the Georgia Experience. *Journal of Criminal Law and Criminology*, Volume 74, pp. 661-753.

Baldus, D.C., Woodworth, G., Zuckerman, D., Weiner, N.A., and Broffitt, B. 2009. Racial Discrimination and the Death Penalty in the Post-*Furman* Era: An Empirical and Legal Overview, with Recent Findings from Philadelphia. *Cornell Law Review*, Volume 83, pp. 1638-1770.

Barker, V., 2009. *The Politics of Imprisonment: How the Democratic Process Shapes the Way America Punishes Offenders.* New York: Oxford University Press.

Barlow, M.H., Barlow, D.E., and Chiricos, T.G., 1995. Mobilizing Support for Social Control in a Declining Economy: Exploring Ideologies of Crime Within Crime News. *Crime and Delinquency*, Volume 41, pp. 191-204.

Beccaria, C., 1777. *An Essay on Crimes and Punishments.* 5th ed. Dublin: John Exshaw.

Beckett, K., 1997. *Making Crime Pay: Law and Order in Contemporary American Politics.* New York: Oxford University Press.

Beckett, K. and Sasson, T., 2000. *The Politics of Injustice: Crime and Punishment in America.* 1st ed. Thousand Oaks (CA): Pine Forge.

Beckett, K. and Sasson, T., 2004. *The Politics of Injustice: Crime and Punishment in America.* 2nd ed. Thousand Oaks (CA): Sage.

Bentele, U. and Bowers, W.J., 2001. How Jurors Decide on Death: Guilt is Overwhelming; Aggravation Requires Death; and Mitigation is No Excuse. *Brooklyn Law Review*, Volume 66, pp. 1011-1339.

Blume, J., Eisenberg, T., and Wells, M., 2004. Explaining Death Row's Population and Racial Composition. *Journal of Empirical Legal Studies*, Volume 1, pp. 165-207.

Bonilla-Silva, E., 2010. *Racism Without Racists: Color-Blind Racism and the Persistence of Racial Inequality in America.* 3rd ed. Lanham, MD: Rowman and Littlefield.

Bowers, W. and Foglia, W., 2007. *Does Hindsight Bias Explain Evidence of Flaws in Capital Jurors Decision-Making?* Atlanta, GA, American Society of Criminology.

Bowers, W.J., 1995. The Capital Jury Project: Rationale, Design, and Preview of Early Findings. *Indiana Law Journal*, Volume 70, pp. 1043-1102.

Bowers, W.J., 1996. The Capital Jury: Is it Tilted Toward Death? *Judicature,* Volume 79, pp. 220-23.

Bowers, W.J., Fleury-Steiner, B.D., and Antonio, M.E., 2003. The Capital Sentencing Decision: Guided Discretion, Reasoned Moral Judgment, or Legal Fiction. In: J.R. Acker, R.M. Bohm, and C.S. Lanier, eds. *America's Experiment with Capital Punishment: Reflection on the Past, Present, and Future of the Ultimate Penal Sanction.* Durham (NC): Carolina Academic Press, pp. 413-68.

Bowers, W.J. and Foglia, W., 2006. *Effects of Memory on Evidence of Problems with Capital Juror Decision-Making.* Los Angeles, CA, American Society of Criminology.

Bowers, W.J., Foglia, W.D., Giles, J.E., and Antonio, M.E., 2006. The Decision Maker Matters: An Empirical Examination of the Way the Role of the Judge and Jury Influence Death Penalty Decision-Making. *Washington and Lee Law Review*, Volume 63, pp. 931-1010.

Bowers, W.J., Sandys, M., and Brewer, T.W., 2003. Crossing Racial Boundaries: A Closer Look at the Roots of Racial Bias When the Defendant is Black and the Victim is White. *DePaul Law Review*, Volume 53, pp. 1497-1538.

Bowers, W.J., Sandys, M., and Steiner, B.D., 1998. Foreclosed Impartiality in Capital Sentencing: Jurors' Predispositions, Guilt-Trial Experience, and Premature Decision Making. *Cornell Law Review*, Volume 83, pp. 1476-1556.

Bowers, W.J. and Steiner, B.D., 1999. "Death by Default: An Empirical Demonstration of False and Forced Choices in Capital Sentencing. *Texas Law Review*, Volume 77, pp. 605-717.

Brace, P. and Boyea, B.D., 2007. Judicial Selection Methods and Capital Punishment in the American States. In: M.J. Streb, ed. *Running for Judge: The Rising Political, Financial, and Legal Stakes of Judicial Elections.* New York: New York University Press, pp. 186-203.

Brake, M. and Hale, C., 1992. *Public Order and Private Lives: The Politics of Law and Order.* New York: Routledge.

Brewer, T.W., 2004. Race and Jurors' Receptivity to Mitigation in Capital Cases: The Effect of Jurors', Defendants', and Victims' Race in Combination. *Law and Human Behavior*, Volume 28, pp. 529-45.

Brooks, R.R. and Raphael, S., 2003. Life Terms or Death Sentences: The Uneasy Relationship Between Judicial Elections and Capital Punishment. *Journal of Criminal Law and Criminology,* Volume 92, pp. 609-40.

Brown, M.K. et al., 2003. *Whitewashing Race: The Myth of a Color-Blind Society.* Berkeley, CA: University of California Press.

Bruno, P.J., 2010. The Mitigation Specialist. *The Champion*, Volume 34, pp. 26-9.

California v. Brown, 479 U.S. 538 (1987).

Callins v. Collins, 510 U.S. 1141 (1994).

CBS DC, 2012. *NRA: 'Only Way To Stop A Bad Guy With A Gun Is A Good Guy With A Gun'.* [Online] Available at: http://washington.cbslocal.com/2012/12/21/nra-only-way-to-stop-a-bad-guy-with-a-gun-is-with-a-good-guy-with-a-gun/.

Cheng, J., 2010. Frontloading Mitigation: The "Legal" and the "Human" in Death Penalty Defense. *Law and Social Inquiry*, Volume 35, pp. 39-65.

Chermak, S.M., 1994. Body Count News: How Crime is Presented in the News Media. *Justice Quarterly*, Volume 11, pp. 561-82.

Cohen, A.K., 1955. *Delinquent Boys: The Culture of the Gang.* Glencoe, IL: Free Press.

Comaroff, J. and Comaroff, J., 1991. *Of Revelation and Revolution.* Chicago: University of Chicago Press.

Condit, C.M. and Selzer, J.A., 1985. The Rhetoric of Objectivity in Newspaper Coverage of a Murder Trial. *Critical Studies in Mass Communication,* Volume 2, pp. 197-216.

Cullen, F.T., Clark, G.A., Cullen, J.B., and Mathers, R.A., 1985. Attribution, Salience, and Attitudes Toward Criminal Sanctioning. *Criminal Justice and Behavior*, Volume 12, pp. 305-31.

Death Penalty Information Center, 2013a. *Recent Legislative Activity.* [Online] Available at: http://www.deathpenaltyinfo.org/recent-legislative-activity [Accessed 2 July 2013].

Death Penalty Information Center, 2013b. *States With and Without the Death Penalty.* [Online] Available at: http://www.deathpenaltyinfo.org/states-and-without-death-penalty [Accessed 2 July 2013].

Delaware State Courts, n.d. *Superior Court: Join our team: Judicial appointments.* [Online] Available at: http://courts.delaware.gov/Superior/AboutUs/team_judges.stm [Accessed 6 August 2012].

Donohue, J.J., 2011. *Capital punishment in Connecticut, 1973-2007: A comprehensive evaluation from 4686 murders to one execution.* [Online] Available at: http://works.bepress.com/john_donohue/87/ [Accessed 9 January 2012].

Dunn, K. and Kaplan, P.J., 2009. The Ironies of Helping: Social Interventions and Executable Subjects. *Law and Society Review*, Volume 43, pp. 337-68.

Eddings v. Oklahoma, 455 U.S. 104 (1982).

Ellis, R., 1993. *American Political Cultures.* New York: Oxford University Press.

Ericson, R., Baranek, P., and Chan, J., 1991. *Representing Order: Crime, Law, and Justice in the News.* Toronto: University of Toronto Press.

Ewick, P. and Silbey, S.S., 1995. Subversive Stories and Hegemonic Tales: Toward a Sociology of Narrative. *Law and Society Review*, Volume 29, pp. 197-226.

Fitzgerald, R. and Ellsworth, P.C., 1984. Due Process vs. Crime Control: Death Qualification and Jury Attitudes. *Law and Human Behavior*, Volume 8, pp. 31-51.

Flanagan, T., 1987. Change and Influence in Popular Criminology: Public Attributions of Crime Causation. *Journal of Criminal Justice*, Volume 15, pp. 231-43.

Fleury-Steiner, B., 2002. Narratives of the Death Sentence: Toward a Theory of Legal Narrativity. *Law and Society Review*, Volume 36, pp. 549-76.

Fleury-Steiner, B., 2004. *Jurors' Stories of Death: How America's Death Penalty Invests in Inequality.* Ann Arbor, MI: University of Michigan Press.

Fleury-Steiner, B.D., Dunn, K., and Fleury-Steiner, R., 2009. Governing Through Crime as Commonsense Racism: Race, Space, and Death Penalty "Reform" in Delaware. *Punishment and Society*, Volume 11, pp. 5-24.

Freedman, E.M., 2008. Introduction: Re-stating the Standard of Practice for Death Penalty Counsel: The Supplementary Guidelines for the Mitigation Function of Defense Teams in Death Penalty Cases. *Hofstra Law Review*, Volume 36, pp. 663-76.

Furman v. Georgia, 408 U.S. 238 (1972).

Galanter, M., 1974. Why the "Haves" Come out Ahead: Speculations on the Limits of Legal Change. *Law and Society Review*, Volume 9, pp. 95-160.

Garden v. State, 815 A.2d 327 (Del., 2003).

Garland, D., 1990. *Punishment and Modern Society: A Study in Social Theory.* Chicago, IL: University of Chicago Press.

Garland, D., 2001. *The Culture of Control: Crime and Social Order in Contemporary Society.* Chicago, IL: University of Chicago Press.

Garvey, S.P., 1998. Aggravation and Mitigation in Capital Cases: What Do Jurors Think? *Columbia Law Review*, Volume 98, pp. 1538-76.

Givelber, D. and Farrell, A., 2012. *Not Guilty: Are the Acquitted Innocent?* New York: New York University Press.

Gorelick, S.M., 1989. "Join Our War": The Construction of Ideology in a Newspaper Crimefighting Campaign. *Journal of Crime and Delinquency*, Volume 35, pp. 421-36.

Gramsci, A., 1971. *Selections from the Prison Notebooks of Antonio Gramsci.* London: Lawrence and Wishart.

Gregg v. Georgia, 428 U.S. 153 (1976).

Guthrie, C., Rachlinski, J.J., and Wistrich, A.J., 2001. Inside the Judicial Mind. *Cornell Law Review*, Volume 86, pp. 777-830.

Haney, C., 1982. Criminal Justice and the Ninteenth-Century Paradigm: The Triumph of Psychological Individualism in the "Formative Era." *Law and Human Behavior*, Volume 6, pp. 191-235.

Haney, C., 1984. On the Selection of Capital Juries: The Biasing Effects of the Death-Qualification Process. *Law and Human Behavior*, Volume 8, pp. 121-32.

Haney, C., 1995. The Social Context of Capital Murder: Social Histories and the Logic of Mitigation. *Santa Clara Law Review*, Volume 35, pp. 547-609.

Haney, C., 1997. Commonsense Justice and Capital Punishment: Problematizing the "Will of the People." *Psychology, Public Policy, and Law*, Volume 3, pp. 303-37.

Haney, C., 2003. Mitigation and the Study of Lives: On the Roots of Violent Criminality and the Nature of Capital Justice. In: J.R. Acker, R.M. Bohm, and C.S. Lanier, eds. *America's Experiment with Capital Punishment: Reflections on the Past, Present, and Future of the Ultimate Penal Sanction.* Durham, NC: Carolina Academic Press, pp. 469-500.

Haney, C., 2004. Condemning the Other in Death Penalty Trials: Biographical Racism, Structural Mitigation, and the Empathetic Divide. *DePaul Law Review*, Volume 53, pp. 1557-89.

Haney, C., 2005. *Death by Design: Capital Punishment as a Social Psychological System.* New York: Oxford University Press.

Haney, C. and Greene, S., 2004. Capital Constructions: Newspaper Reporting in Death Penalty Cases. *Analyses of Social Issues and Public Policy,* Volume 4, pp. 129-150.

Haney, C. and Lynch, M., 1994. Comprehending Life and Death Matters: A Preliminary Study of California's Capital Penalty Instructions. *Law and Human Behavior*, Volume 18, pp. 411-46.

Haney, C. and Lynch, M., 1997. Clarifying Life and Death Matters: An Analysis of Instructional Comprehension and Penalty Phase Closing Arguments. *Law and Human Behavior*, Volume 21, pp. 575-95.

Haney, C., Sontag, L., and Costanzo, S., 1994. Deciding to Take a Life: Capital Juries, Sentencing Instructions, and the Jurisprudence of Death. *Journal of Social Issues*, Volume 50, pp. 149-76.

Hoffman, J.L., 1997. How American Juries Decide Death Penalty Cases: The Capital Jury Project. In: H.A. Bedau, ed. *The Death Penalty in America: Current Controversies.* New York: Oxford University Press, pp. 333-43.

Holdman, S. and Seeds, C., 2008. Imagining Mitigation: Cultural Competency in Capital Mitigation. *Hofstra Law Review*, Volume 36, pp. 883-922.

Holmes, J.O.W., 1881. *The Common Law.* Boston, MA: Little, Brown and Company.

Howard, M., 2004. *Full text: Michael Howard's Speech on Crime.* [Online] Available at: http://www.guardian.co.uk/politics/2004/aug/10/conservatives.speeches [Accessed 28 September 2009].

Humphries, D., 1981. Serious Crime, News Coverage, and Ideology: A Content Analysis of Crime Coverage in a Metropolitan Paper. *Crime and Delinquency*, Volume 27, pp. 191-205.

Hurst, J.W., 1956. *Law and the Conditions of Freedom in the Nineteenth Century United States.* Madison, WI: University of Wisconsin Press.

Johnson, S.L. et al., 2012. The Delaware death penalty: An empirical study. *Iowa Law Review*, Volume 97, pp. 1925-64.

Kalven, H.J. and Zeisel, H., 1966. *The American Jury.* Chicago: University of Chicago Press.

Keller, H., 1968. *Midstream: My Later Life.* New York: Greenwood.

Kleinstuber, R., 2013. "Only a Recommendation": How Delaware Capital Sentencing Law Subverts Meaningful Deliberations and Jurors' Feelings of Responsibility. *Widener Law Review,* Volume 19(2), pp. 321-44.

Landsman, S. and Rakos, R.F., 1994. A Preliminary Inquiry into the Effect of Potentially Biasing Information on Judges and Jurors in Civil Litigation. *Behavioral Sciences and the Law*, Volume 12, pp. 113-26.

Lenza, M., Keys, D., and Guess, T., 2005. The Prevailing Injustices in the Application of the Missouri Death Penalty (1978 to 1996). *Social Justice*, Volume 32(2), pp. 151-66.

Lockett v. Ohio, 438 U.S. 586 (1978).

Loeber, R. and Farrington, D.P. eds., 2001. *Child Delinquents: Development, Intervention, and Service Needs.* Thousand Oaks(CA): Sage.

Loewen, J.W., 1995. *Lies My Teacher Told Me: Everything Your American History Textbook Got Wrong.* New York: Touchstone.

Lynch, M. and Haney, C., 2000. Discrimination and Instructional Comprehension: Guided Discretion, Racial Bias, and the Death Penalty. *Law and Human Behavior*, Volume 24, pp. 337-56.

Lyon, A.F., 2004. Naming the Dragon: Litigating Race Issues During a Death Penalty Trial. *DePaul Law Review*, Volume 53, pp. 1647-61.

McCleskey v. Kemp, 481 U.S. 279 (1987).

Mansley, E.A., 2009. *Intimate Partner Violence: Race, Social Class, and Masculinity.* El Paso, TX: LFB Scholarly.

Morgan v. Illinois, 504 U.S. 719 (1992).

Oliver, M.L. and Shapiro, T.M., 1995. *Black Wealth/White Wealth: A New Perspective on Racial Inequality.* New York: Routledge.

Palin, S., 2011. *America's Enduring Strength.* [Online] Available at: http://www.facebook.com/note.php?note_id=487510653434.

Paternoster, R. and Brame, R., 2008. Reassessing Race Disparities in Maryland Capital Cases. *Criminology*, Volume 46, pp. 971-1008.

Penry v. Lynaugh, 492 U.S. 302 (1989).

Pierce, G.L. and Radelet, M., 2005. The impact of legally inappropriate factors on death sentencing for California homicides, 1990-1999. *Santa Clara Law Review*, Volume 46, pp. 1-47.

Pinello, D., 1995. *The Impact of Judicial-Selection Method on State-Supreme-Court Policy: Innovation, Reaction, and Atrophy.* Westport, CT: Greenwood.

Pratt, T.C. et al., 2008. The Empirical Status of Deterrence Theory: A Meta-Analysis. In: F.T. Cullen, J.P. Wright, and K.R. Blevins, eds. *Taking Stock: The Status of Criminological Theory.* New Brunswick, NJ: Transaction, pp. 367-95.

Riessman, C.K., 1993. *Narrative Analysis.* Newbury Park, CA: Sage.

Rini, J., 2013a. *House Panel Tables Death Penalty Repeal Bill.* [Online] Available at:http://delaware.newszap.com/centraldelaware/122003-70/house-panel-tables-death-penalty-repeal-bill [Accessed 26 August 2013].

Rini, J., 2013b. *Supporters of Delaware Death Penalty Repeal Vow to Fight On.* [Online] Available at: http://delaware.newszap.com/centraldelaware/121969-70/supporters-of-delaware-death-penalty-repeal-vow-to-fight-on [Accessed 26 August 2013].

Rise Against, 2011. *Disparity by Design.* [Sound Recording] (DGC Records).

Rompilla v. Beard, 545 U.S. 374 (2005).

Roper v. Simmons, 543 U.S. 551 (2005).

Said, E.W., 1978. *Orientalism.* New York: Vintage.

Samenow, S.E., 2004. *Inside the Criminal Mind.* Revised and Updated ed. New York: Crown.

Sandys, M. and McClelland, S., 2003. Stacking the Deck for Guilt and Death: The Failure of Death Qualification to Ensure Impartiality. In: J.R. Acker, R.M. Bohm, and C.S. Lanier, eds. *America's Experiment with Capital Punishment: Reflection on the Past, Present, and Future of the Ultimate Penal Sanction.* 2nd ed. Durham (NC): Carolina Academic Press, pp. 385-412.

Sarat, A., 1995. Violence, Representation, and Responsibility in Capital Trials: The View From the Jury. *Indiana Law Journal,* Volume 70, pp. 1103-60.

Sarat, A., 2001. *When the State Kills: Capital Punishment and the American Condition.* Princeton, NJ: Princeton University Press.

Sarat, A., 2005. *Mercy on Trial: What It Means to Stop an Execution.* Princeton, NJ: Princeton University Press.

Sasson, T., 1995. *Crime Talk: How Citizens Construct a Social Problem.* New York: Aldine de Gruyter.

Scheingold, S.A., 1984. *The Politics of Law and Order: Street Crime and Public Policy.* New York: Longman.

Scheingold, S.A., 1991. *The Politics of Street Crime: Criminal Process and Cultural Obsession.* Philadelphia, PA: Temple University Press.

Scott, M. and Lyman, S., 1968. Accounts. *American Sociological Review,* Volume 33, pp. 46-62.

Shahid, A., 2011. *Herman Cain to Occupy Wall Street protesters: If you're not rich 'blame yourself'.* [Online] Available at: http://www.nydailynews.com/news/politics/herman-cain-occupy-wall-street-protesters-rich-blame-article-1.961517.

Spence, T.R., 2003. *Delaware House Bill #287. An Act to Amend Title 11 of the Delaware Code Relating to the Classification of Offenses, Sentences.* [Online] Available at: http://legis.delaware.gov/LIS/lis142.nsf/93487d394bc01014882569a4007a4cb7/727a8ed0650c197485256d4f00686235?OpenDocument [Accessed 30 November 2009].

Strauss, A.L., 1987. *Qualitative Analysis for Social Scientists.* New York: Cambridge University Press.

Sundby, S.E., 1997. The Jury as Critic: An Empirical Look at How Capital Juries Perceive Expert and Lay Testimony. *Virginia Law Review*, Volume 83, pp. 1109-88.

Surette, R., 1998. *Media, Crime, and Criminal Justice.* Belmont, CA: Wadsworth.

Surette, R., and Richard, A., 1995. Public Information Officers: A Descriptive Study of Crime News Gatekeepers. *Journal of Criminal Justice*, Volume 23, pp. 325-36.

Sutherland, E.H., 1947. *Principles of Criminology*. 4th ed. Philadelphia, PA: Lippincott.

Tennard v. Dretke (2004).

Tiersma, P.M., 1995. Dictionaries and Death: Do Capital Jurors Understand Mitigation? *Utah Law Review*, pp. 1-49.

Urbina, M.G., 2003. Race and Ethnic Differences in Punishment and Death Sentence Outcomes: Empirical Analysis of Data on California, Florida and Texas, 1975-1995. *Journal of Ethnicity in Criminal Justice*, Volume 1, pp. 5-35.

Vago, S., 2012. *Law and Society*. Upper Saddle River, NJ: Pearson.

Vartkessian, E.S., 2011. Dangerously Biased: How the Texas Capital Sentencing Statute Encourages Jurors To Be Unreceptive to Mitigation Evidence. *Quinnipiac Law Review*, Volume 29, pp. 237-88.

Vartkessian, E.S., 2012. What One Hand Giveth, The Other Taketh Away: How Future Dangerousness Corrupts Guilt Verdicts and Produces Premature Punishment Decisions in Capital Cases. *Pace Law Review*, Volume 32, pp. 447-87.

Wasserman, G.A. et al., 2003. Risk and Protective Factors of Juvenile Delinquency. *Child Delinquency Bulletin Series*, April.

Webster, C., 2008. Marginalized White Ethnicity, Race and Crime. *Theoretical Criminology*, Volume 12, pp. 293-312.

Wiggins v. Smith, 539 U.S. 510 (2003).

Williams v. Taylor, 529 U.S. 362 (2000).

Wilson, J.Q., 1975. *Thinking About Crime*. New York: Basic.

Wistrich, A.J., Guthrie, C., and Rachlinski, J.J., 2005. Can Judges Ignore Inadmissible Information? The Difficulty of Deliberately Disregarding. *University of Pennsylvania Law Review*, Volume 153, pp. 1251-1345.

Wolfgang, M.E. and Ferracuti, F., 1967. *The Subculture of Violence: Towards an Integrated Theory in Criminology*. London: Tavistock.

Woodson v. North Carolina, 428 U.S. 280 (1976).

Young, R.L., 2004. Guilty Until Proven Innocent: Conviction Orientation, Racial Attitudes, and Support for Capital Punishment. *Deviant Behavior*, Volume 25, pp. 151-67.

Index

For Product Safety Concerns and Information please contact our EU
representative GPSR@taylorandfrancis.com
Taylor & Francis Verlag GmbH, Kaufingerstraße 24, 80331 München, Germany

www.ingramcontent.com/pod-product-compliance
Ingram Content Group UK Ltd.
Pitfield, Milton Keynes, MK11 3LW, UK
UKHW020205200926
475702UK00004B/618
9781472425591